The First Book of

Microsoft® Works
for Windows™

The First Book of

Microsoft® Works
for Windows™

Clayton Walnum

SAMS

A Division of Prentice Hall Computer Publishing
11711 North College, Carmel, Indiana 46032 USA

To Stu Wing, a hacker in training.

International Standard Book Number: 0-672-27374-8
Library of Congress Catalog Card Number: 90-75711

95 94   10 9 8 7

Interpretation of the printing code: the rightmost double-digit number is the year of the book's printing; the rightmost single-digit number, the number of the book's printing. For example, a printing code of 91-1 shows that the first printing of the book occurred in 1991.

Printed in the United States of America

Publisher
Richard K. Swadley

Publishing Manager
Marie Butler-Knight

Managing Editor
Majorie Hopper

Acquisitions/Development Editor
Mary-Terese Cozzola Cagnina

Technical Editor
C. Herbert Feltner

Manuscript Editor
Ronda Carter Henry

Cover Designer
Held & Diedrich Design

Designer
Scott Cook

Indexer
John Sleeva

Production Team
*Jeff Baker, Claudia Bell, Brad Chinn, Brook Farling, Denny Hager,
Audra Hershman, Bob LaRoche, Laurie A. Lee, Linda Seifert,
Dennis Sheehan, Kevin Spear, Mary Beth Wakefield, Lisa Wilson*

**Special thanks to C. Herbert Feltner for assuring the
technical accuracy of this book**

Contents

X

xii

Introduction

Microsoft's Works for Windows is an outstanding value. For the price of a single software package, you get all the major tools you need to become productive on your PC. Whether you're a home user or the owner of a small business, Works for Windows will allow you to create sophisticated word processor, spreadsheet, and database documents.

Works for Windows is amazingly easy to use, but like any complex software package, there's much to learn in order to become proficient with each Works tool. This book is designed to get you up and running with Works for Windows as quickly as possible. Without bogging you down in a lot of unnecessary detail, we guide you through all of Works' major functions, providing not only complete operational instructions, but also application ideas and examples.

How to Use This Book

How you use this book depends largely upon the experience you've had with other software, particularly software designed for the Windows operating system. While this book covers Works for Windows' functions in detail, it does assume that you're familiar with Windows. In this book, we quickly review the main operations involved in handling windows, dialog boxes, and menus. However, this book is in no way a guide to using Windows.

Therefore, if you're not familiar with the Windows operating system, before attempting to use Works for Windows (or any other Windows software package), you should take some time to learn the basics of the Windows user interface. The time spent will help you not only with Works for Windows, but also with most other Windows-compatible software.

Once you're comfortable with Windows, read Chapter 1, "Getting Started" and Chapter 2, "Common Works for Windows File Functions." These chapters introduce you to the tools included with Works for Windows, as well as offer a look at some basic Windows operating procedures needed for manipulating the programs. You'll use what you learn in these introductory chapters throughout the rest of the book.

Finally, select the tool you want to learn—the word processor, the database, the spreadsheet, or Microsoft Draw—and turn to that section of the book. We've dedicated two or three chapters to each tool (except Microsoft Draw, which has only one chapter), with major functions like printing and charting given chapters of their own. There's no need to read this book from cover to cover. In fact, the time spent in such a reading would be, at first, mostly wasted. You'll learn best by doing. Learn enough to get started with a particular tool, and then get to work. When you need to learn a new function, find the appropriate section in the book. In this way you'll quickly learn what you need to know, saving the "icing" for later.

Conventions Used in This Book

To help you find material quickly, we've used the following icons to identify important functions and hints:

Quick Steps provide step-by-step instructions for performing most major Works' functions. If a particular function is at all complicated, you'll find a Quick Step to help you along. To help you quickly locate the most common operations, an index of Quick Steps is listed on the inside front cover of this book.

 This icon identifies handy tips that make using Works more enjoyable and productive. It also indicates notes, which provide additional information about a tool or tool function, giving you greater understanding of how that tool or function operates.

You'll find several warnings throughout this book, each of which identifies functions or procedures that could damage your data or computer system if used improperly.

Because Works for Windows is an integrated software package, the tools incorporate many of the same functions. Rather than repeat a lot of information in each section of the book, the common operations icon points you to where important operations were previously covered in the book.

This icon identifies special task-oriented tips for using Works at home or in your business.

XV

Of Mice and Keyboards

As we said before, it is necessary for you to become familiar with Windows in order to run Works easily. While we can't provide a complete guide to Windows, we have compiled a list of frequently used Windows commands. While you can operate Windows programs solely from the keyboard, we advise that you invest in a mouse, if you haven't already. Some Windows operations are cumbersome to employ from the keyboard.

Still, in order to keep this book helpful to both mouse and keyboard users, we've tried to include the information either would require to operate Works. Whenever you see the word *select* or *choose* in this book, you should use one of these operations.

Selecting a menu

Mouse: Click on the menu's name.

Keyboard: Hold down Alt and press the underlined letter in the menu's name.

Selecting a menu entry

Mouse: Click on the entry.

Keyboard: Press the entry's underlined letter.

Selecting a button in a dialog box

Mouse: Click on the button.

Keyboard: Hold down Alt and press the underlined letter on the button. For buttons that have no underlined letter, press Tab until the button is selected, and then press Enter.

Selecting a field in a dialog box

Mouse: Click on the field.

Keyboard: Press Tab until the field is selected.

Selecting an option from a group in a dialog box

Mouse: Click on the option.

Keyboard: Hold down Alt and press the option's underlined letter. If the option has no underlined letter, press Tab until the group is selected, use your arrow keys to highlight the option, and then press the spacebar to activate it.

If you've never used a mouse before, some of the terms we used in the above commands may be new to you. Following is a list of mouse terms we use in this book.

Click: Place the mouse pointer over the item and quickly press the left mouse button once.

Double-click: Place the mouse pointer over the item and press the left mouse button twice in rapid succession.

Drag: Place the mouse pointer over the item, hold down the left mouse button, and move the pointer across the screen.

Acknowledgments

I would like to thank the following people for their contributions to this book:

 Mary-Terese Cagnina for her invaluable guidance.

▶ Ronda Henry for making the words right.

- C. Herbert Feltner for checking the details.
- Stuart Wing for continually reminding me of my deadlines.
- Mary-Lou Rouviere and Paul Dubay for providing a place to crash on Saturday nights.
- Anne Kichar for babysitting and ego boosting.
- My wife, Lynn, and my sons, Christopher, Justin, and Stephen, without whom I'd be nothing.

Trademark Acknowledgments

Microsoft, Toolbar, and Windows are registered trademarks of Microsoft Corporation. All other product and service names are trademarks and service marks of their respective owners.

Getting Started

In This Chapter

▶ *Starting Works for Windows*
▶ *The Works for Windows Tools*
▶ *Selecting tools*
▶ *Getting help*
▶ *Quitting Works for Windows*

Like most integrated software packages (packages that feature several interrelated programs), Works for Windows is a complex system. In this chapter, you'll be introduced to the Works tools and learn basic Works operations, such as starting the program, starting the different tools, and exiting back to Windows. Once you learn basic terms and procedures, you'll be ready to experiment with the programs themselves and take advantage of the many functions they provide.

Starting Works for Windows

When Works is installed, it creates a program group called Microsoft Solution Series, as shown in Figure 1.1. You'll find the Works for

Windows program icon in this window. To start Works, double-click on the Microsoft Works program icon. Alternatively, you can click on the Microsoft Works program icon, and then press Enter to run it.

Keyboard users must press Alt+W to access the Window menu. Then press the down arrow to move the highlight in the menu to the group in which Works is located. Press Enter when the proper group is highlighted. If the group doesn't appear in the menu, select More Windows and the group from the dialog box that appears. After selecting the program group, use the direction arrows to select Works in the window, and then press Enter to start it.

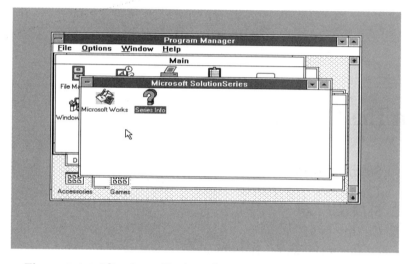

Figure 1.1   After installation, the Microsoft Works program icon will be in the Microsoft Solution Series program group.

> **Note:** If you have not yet installed Works for Windows, turn to Appendix A "Installation," for complete instructions.

The Works for Windows Tools

Works for Windows is actually five programs in one, including a *word processor,* a *spreadsheet,* a *database,* a *drawing program,* and *WorksWizards,* a sort of electronic assistant that helps you create labels, form letters, and even electronic address books. These tools are excellent for both business and home use, letting you write letters, keep track of finances, create mailing lists, print labels and forms, and much more. Below is a brief look at each tool and how it can be used.

The Word Processor

Before the arrival of personal computers, letters and other documents had to be created on a typewriter. This could be a long and laborious process, because making corrections often meant retyping an entire document. A word processor allows you to create a document on your computer's screen. This document is then saved to a disk file, from which it can be retrieved any time. Because this "electronic" document is nothing more than a bunch of numbers in your computer's memory—numbers that your computer can easily shuffle around—making corrections and changes, even major ones, is fairly easy. When your document is exactly the way you want it, you can then print one or more copies with your printer.

The Works word processor is essentially a stripped-down version of Microsoft's high-end word processor, Word for Windows. Although the Works word processor is missing many features found in Word for Windows, it's still a powerful program, one that can handle just about any type of document you may need to create. The Works word processor allows you to change fonts and character sizes; add graphics to your documents; check your spelling; find synonyms; create headers, footers, and footnotes; modify your page layouts; and even print form letters and mailing labels.

In addition, data from other Works tools can be easily incorporated into your documents. For example, you can automatically add a list of addresses to your document by merging data from the database, or you can add a financial report to a letter by merging data from the spreadsheet. You can even spice up your reports by adding charts and graphs, which are generated automatically by the

3

spreadsheet. If you want to be sure that a document containing a report or chart is always updated, you can link the document to the spreadsheet. Then, when you change the spreadsheet's data, your document is automatically updated. Unless you have unusual needs, the Works word processor can handle just about any word-processing task you can think of. Figure 1.2 shows a document created with the Works word processor.

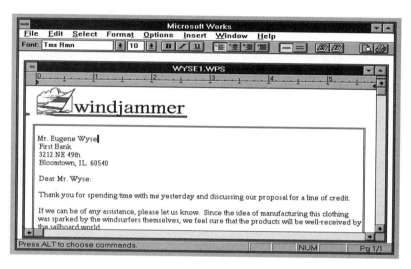

Figure 1.2 The Works word processor is a powerful tool for creating sophisticated documents.

Microsoft Draw

Although Microsoft Draw, the drawing program that comes with Works, is not a free-standing application like the word processor, database, and spreadsheet (it can be loaded only from within the word processor and has no way to save its drawings except by merging them into your document), it's still a full-fledged program that can handle virtually any of your graphics needs. Unlike a paint program, Microsoft Draw creates graphics by combining objects—including rectangles, arcs, circles, and lines. Each object is a separate entity that can be manipulated individually. For example, you can place a rectangle over a circle, while still being able to "pick up" and move the circle. Objects are laid on the screen, much like slips of colored paper, and combined into whatever shapes you like.

You can change the color of any object at any time, even set an object's border and interior to different colors. Once you've come up with a shape you like, you can combine its objects and move it around as one piece. You can add text to your drawings, create objects from many types of patterns and lines, modify any color in the palette, import pictures from other programs, and zoom in on a drawing in order to see it in greater detail.

If you're used to paint programs, which treat the entire screen as a single object, you may have to experiment to become proficient at creating drawings with Microsoft Draw. But once you get the hang of it, you'll appreciate the power of object-oriented graphics. Figure 1.3 shows objects created in the Works drawing program.

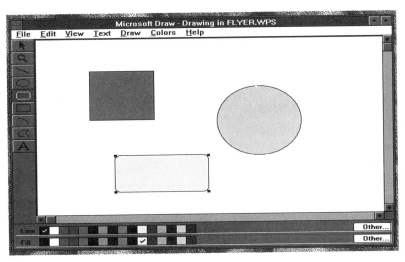

Figure 1.3   Microsoft Draw uses an object-oriented approach to creating graphics.

Note: You can start Microsoft Draw only from within the word processor, by selecting <u>D</u>rawing from the Insert pull-down menu.

5

The Database

Using the Works database, you can do everything from creating a Christmas card list to setting up an accounts receivable file. When you start a new database, you define a record made up of various fields. For example, for an accounts receivable database, you might create a record which would include the name, address, phone number, balance, and payment fields. You'd then use this "template" to enter a record for each of your customers. After entering the customer data, you could command Works to search for any information you may need to find. You could, for example, search for a specific customer or create a list of all customers who live in a certain city. You could even combine search criteria, which would allow you to find all customers who live in a certain city and who have account balances larger or smaller than a specified amount.

Once you create a Works database, you can manipulate the data in many ways. You can easily add, delete, or move fields; edit entries; sort records; print the database; or change field sizes. You can even install default entries for fields. For example, if most customers in your accounts receivable database live in Hartford, CT, you can have this information automatically entered into every record. You then need only change records of customers who live elsewhere.

Of course, you can add database data into your word processor documents. Addresses stored in your databases, for example, can be used to create form letters and mailing labels. The database also has powerful reporting features. You decide which fields to include in a report and where they will be printed. You can add text and labels, create page breaks between certain types of records, and even total numerical fields. Figure 1.4 illustrates the Works database.

The Spreadsheet

A spreadsheet program allows you to create documents that contain many numbers and calculations, so it's especially useful for keeping track of financial information. Basically, a spreadsheet is made up of rows and columns of *cells.* A cell may contain text, a formula, or a value. When you change one value, any values related to it are automatically recalculated. Spreadsheets can handle all types of documents, from packing list forms to financial statements.

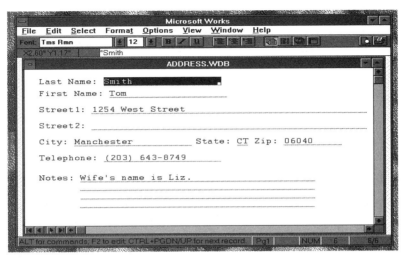

Figure 1.4   The Works database allows you to create an electronic filing system.

7

For example, suppose you need to keep track of business expenses. You could first type into a column of cells the name of each expense. Then in the cells next to the name, you'd enter the balance owed and the monthly payment. Below the balance-owed column, you'd enter a formula that totals all the values in the column, giving you a total owed. Below the monthly-payment column, you'd enter a formula that totals all the payments, telling you how much per month you need to pay your expenses.

The spreadsheet can create a variety of charts based on the values you enter. Line graphs, bar graphs, and pie charts are some ways you can graphically represent the data in your spreadsheet. These charts can be added to documents created in the word processor, enabling you to design sophisticated reports. Figure 1.5 shows the Works spreadsheet.

WorksWizards

WorksWizards are scripts (lists of instructions) that automatically create mailing labels, form letters, and address books. By using WorksWizards, you can create these common documents easily, without having to wade through a lot of documentation. Each WorksWizard guides you with on-screen instructions, prompting you for the information it needs to create the type of document you chose. After you've given a WorksWizard the information it needs to do its job, it then acts as a kind of ghost user, performing all the commands required to create your document. You can actually watch a WorksWizard select menus, answer prompts, position text, and so on, doing all the things you'd have to do to complete the same task. Using WorksWizards, you can be productive with Works almost immediately. Figure 1.6 shows the opening screen of the Form Letters WorksWizard.

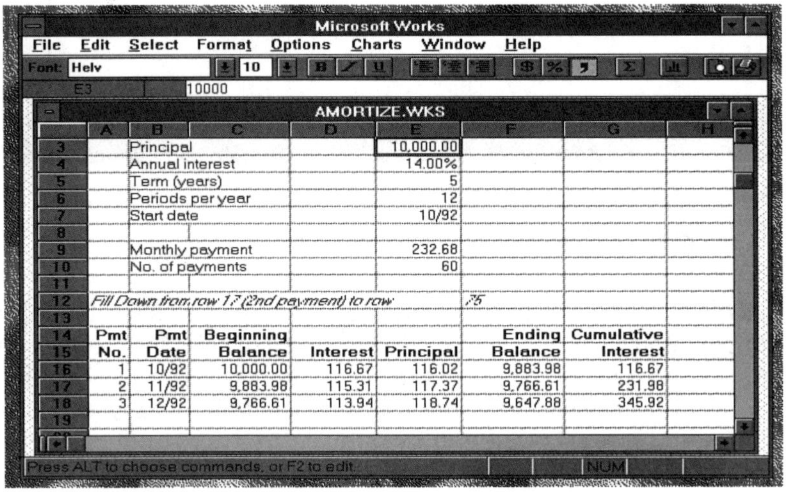

8

Figure 1.5   The Works spreadsheet can handle complicated, math-intensive documents.

Selecting a Tool

When you first run Works, you'll see the Startup dialog box (Figure 1.7), which enables you to start a tool or load a previously created file. To start a tool, select the Word Processor, Spreadsheet, Database, or WorksWizards button. The selected tool then runs and automatically opens a new document window for you. For practice, load the spreadsheet tool. Click on the icon or press Alt+S, and the spreadsheet tool loads, displaying a new worksheet in the document window (Figure 1.8).

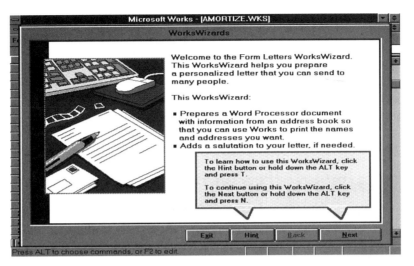

Figure 1.6   WorksWizards help create mailing labels, form letters, and address books.

9

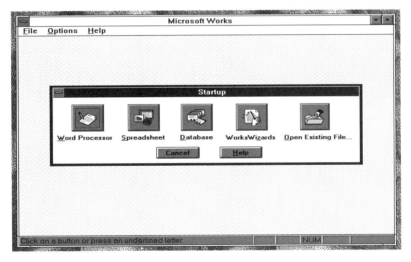

Figure 1.7   You can start any tool you like from the Startup dialog box.

The Works screen is divided into several parts, as shown in Figure 1.8. The *Menu bar* provides access to all of a tool's functions. The *Toolbar,* which varies in appearance from tool to tool, offers fast selection of some frequently used functions. Below the Toolbar is the *document window,* which displays your documents and is where you'll do most of your work. Below the document window, at the bottom of the screen, is the *Status bar,* which displays information about your document and messages from Works. Each tool's screen layout is similar, with only minor differences between them.

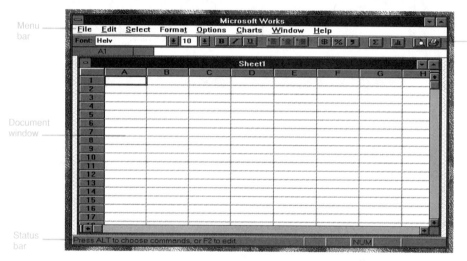

Figure 1.8 *A new worksheet is displayed when you load the spreadsheet tool.*

Getting Help

This book should answer most of the questions you have about Works for Windows, but if you get confused about how some part of Works operates, you can take advantage of the program's extensive help system. To get help, select Help from the Works Menu bar. The Help pull-down menu appears, from which you can select an appropriate topic, as shown in Figure 1.9. The help topics offered vary depending on the tool you're using. All tools, however, offer help on basic usage and keyboard shortcuts, as well as access to the Works tutorial, which guides you step-by-step through each tool. Some dialog boxes also provide help, via a Help button. Select the Help button, and specific instructions for the dialog box appear.

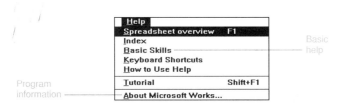

Program information

Basic help

Figure 1.9   The Help menu offers several ways to get the information you need.

 Note: To help you get started, Works provides an on-screen tutorial, which can be accessed by selecting Help from the Menu bar, and then selecting Tutorial from the Help pull-down menu.

11

Quitting Works for Windows

When you've finished your current task, it's important that you exit Works properly. Failure to follow the correct exiting procedure may cause you to lose important data. *Never* exit Works, or any other program, by turning off your machine. In the best case, you may end up with undeleted temporary files on your disk, which, while they cause no harm, take up valuable storage space. In the worst case, you may turn off your machine while Works for Windows is writing data to your disk. Obviously, this is to be avoided at all costs, since you could leave data errors on your hard drive, as well as lose important data files.

Warning: Never exit Works by shutting off your computer. If you do, you may lose valuable data.

To quit Works, double-click on the Control menu box in the upper left corner of the Works window. Alternatively, if you select the Control menu box, you can display the Control menu from which you can exit Works by selecting C̲lose. You can also just press Alt+F4 on your keyboard. It's a good practice to save any updated files (if you want to save them) before trying to close an application. However, if you should forget to save files, Works reminds you before it closes. Figure 1.10 shows the activated Control menu.

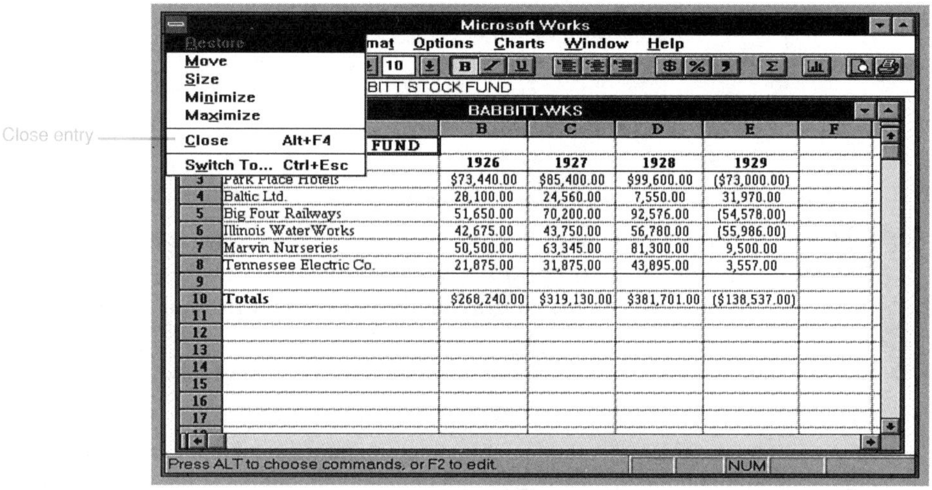

Figure 1.10   You can exit Works by selecting Close from the Control menu.

> **Note:** To exit Works, keyboard users should press Alt+F to access the File menu, and then press **x** to select Exit Works.

What You Have Learned

▶ To start Works from within Windows, double-click on the Microsoft Works program icon.

▶ Works for Windows is made up of five programs that work together, sharing data between them.

▶ The word processor allows you to produce attractive documents that can contain graphics and charts, as well as text.

▶ You can use Microsoft Draw to create object-oriented graphics for your documents.

▶ The Works database lets you set up an electronic filing system.

▶ Using the Works spreadsheet, you can create documents and forms that contain many calculations.

▶ WorksWizards help you create labels, form letters, and electronic address books.

▶ To start a Works tool, select the appropriate button on the Startup dialog box, or press the Alt key and the underlined letter on the button. You also can start a tool by selecting Open Existing File or Create New File in the Works' File menu.

▶ You can get help on just about anything in Works by selecting the Help pull-down menu or by selecting the Help button in a dialog box.

▶ To quit Works, double-click on the Control menu box in the upper left corner of the Works window, or select Exit Works from the File menu.

13

Common Works for Windows File Functions

In This Chapter

▶ *Handling files*
▶ *Viewing a document*
▶ *Navigating the Works for Windows document window*
▶ *Switching between windows*

Because Works for Windows integrates several software tools into one package, there are many functions common to all the programs. These common functions have mainly to do with manipulating files, formatting documents, and printing. Once you learn how to print a simple word processing document, for example, you'll know how to print a simple spreadsheet document too.

Rather than repeating the same instructions for these operations in each tool's section, we'll explain common operations early on, so that you can understand where the program is truly integrated and where modules work independently.

▶ Common file operations are covered in this chapter.
▶ Common formatting operations are covered in Chapter 3, "Word Processor Basics" and Chapter 4, "Advanced Word Processing."
▶ Common printing operations are covered in Chapter 5, "Printing."

In future chapters when we discuss a common operation, a *Common Operations* icon will remind you where the operation is originally covered, so that the chapter can focus on special aspects of the function. For example, when printing is discussed in Chapter 10, "Spreadsheet Basics," it will focus on spreadsheet-specific instances of printing, such as selecting a print area and printing large spreadsheets. A Common Operations icon will direct you to Chapter 5, "Printing," for basic printing information.

Starting a New File

Before you can create any type of document, you must open a new file. This file, which will be located on your hard disk, will hold the contents of your document when you save it. By storing your document in a disk file, you can reload it into Works whenever you need to print or edit it.

Each file is associated with a document window, which appears when you start or load a file. The document window displays your data as you type it, whether that data is the text of a letter, the fields of a database, or the cells of a spreadsheet.

You can start a new file in one of two ways:

▶ By selecting the appropriate tool button on the Startup dialog box (see Figure 2.1).

▶ By selecting Create New File from the File pull-down menu (see Figure 2.2).

In both cases, Works automatically opens and names a document window of the correct type (word processor, database, or spreadsheet). You can then begin work on the new document.

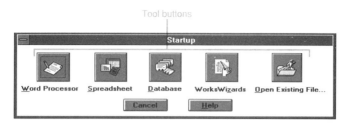

Figure 2.1   You can start a new file by selecting the Word Processor, Database, Spreadsheet, or WorksWizards button on the Startup dialog box.

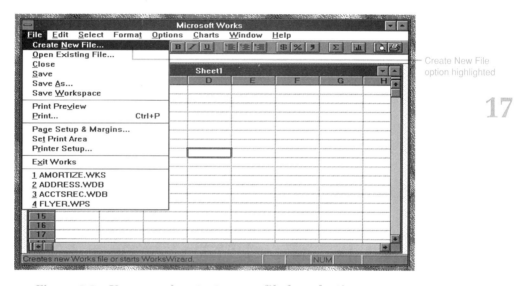

Figure 2.2   You can also start a new file by selecting Create New File in the File menu.

Renaming a File

When Works starts a new file for you, it gives the file a default file name. For example, Works names the first word processor file you open WORD1.WPS or the first spreadsheet file SHEET1.WKS. After you place data in a file, you'll want to change these generic names to something more appropriate, so you can tell by the file name what a file contains. You might, for example, want to name a letter to your friend Carl Smith SMITH.WPS.

To rename a file, select Save As from the File pull-down menu, as detailed in the following Quick Steps.

Renaming a File

1. Make sure the file's window is active. (Click on the window or select the window from the Window pull-down menu.)

   The file's window appears on top of any other Works document windows that may be open.

2. Select Save As from the File pull-down menu.

   The Save As dialog box appears (see Figure 2.3).

3. Type a new file name, eight characters or less in length. (You do not need to type the three-letter extension.)

   The new file name appears in the File Name text box.

4. Press Enter or select the OK button.

   Works saves the file under its new file name.

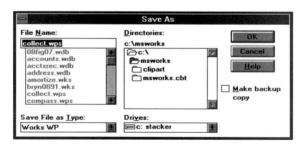

Figure 2.3   The Save As dialog box.

Note: If you've saved a file before renaming it, when the file is saved under a new name, the old file will still exist under the old file name until you delete it.

18

Warning: Because Works reuses the same default file names, be sure to rename a document when saving it for the first time. Otherwise, you may inadvertently save a new document over an old one with the same default name, destroying the old file forever. To be absolutely safe, rename a new document immediately after starting it. When you save a document for the first time, Works reminds you to rename it by bringing up the Save As dialog box.

Closing a Document

Often you may want to close the document you're working on without exiting Works. You may, for example, have finished a letter and now want to work on an outline for a paper. Before closing a document, you must be sure that it has been saved. If you forget to save a document, Works will remind you when you try to close it (see Figure 2.4). If you choose to ignore this reminder, any work done on the document since it was last saved will be lost, so be careful and think about what you're doing.

19

Figure 2.4   A dialog box will remind you to save your file before you close it.

The following Quick Steps detail how to close a document.

Closing an Unsaved Document

1. Make sure the file's window is active. (Click on the window or select the window from the Window pull-down menu.)

   The file's window appears on top of any other Works document windows that may be open.

2. Select Close from the File pull-down menu.

Works asks if you want to save the file.

3. Select the Yes button.

Works saves the file and closes its document window.

You can also close a document by clicking on the upper left corner of the document's window (the Control Menu box), and then selecting the Close option from the pull-down menu that appears. Note that, if you close a document that has not been updated since it was last saved, Works simply closes the document window without resaving the file or asking if you want it saved.

Saving a File

Often, you'll want to save a file and then continue working on it. In fact, it's a good idea to save your work as often as is practical. Then, if your computer loses power, most of your work will have already been safely tucked away in its file, where it can be retrieved after you restart your system.

To save a file without closing it, select Save from the File pull-down menu. Works saves the file, after which you can continue working. If you try to use the Save function before renaming a new file, the Save function will bring up the Save As dialog box.

> **FYIdea:** To avoid losing your work or damaging your computer system during an electrical storm, save and close your file, exit the program you are working in, shut off your computer, and then *unplug* it.

Opening a Document

Once you've created a document and saved it to a disk, you can later load it back into Works. You might, for example, want to do more work on the document, or print out an extra copy. To practice, open the sample file in your WORKS directory called HARDWARE.WPS. You can load an already created document in one of two ways.

▶ When you first run Works, you can select the Open Existing File button in the Startup dialog box. The Open dialog box appears, (see Figure 2.5) from which you can choose a file to load.

▶ You can also load a previously created document by selecting Open Existing File from the File pull-down menu.

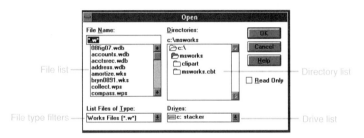

Figure 2.5   The Open dialog box lets you choose which file to load.

21

The following Quick Steps detail these two procedures.

 Opening an Existing Document

1. Select Open Existing File from the File pull-down menu.	The Open dialog box appears.
2. If your file is not stored in the default directory, find the correct directory in the Directories list box and double-click on it. (You can also select the directory name, and then select the OK button.)	Works displays the contents of the new directory in the File Name list box.
3. Find the file you want to open in the file list and double-click on it, or select the file name and then choose the OK button.	A document window appears and Works loads the selected document into it (see Figure 2.6).

> **Note:** Whenever you open an already existing document, Works automatically starts the tool with which the document was created.

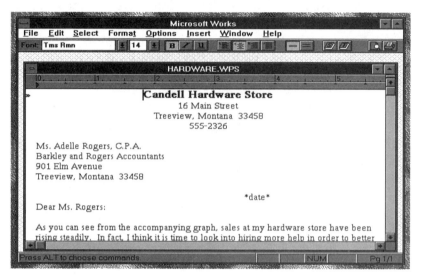

Figure 2.6   The Works file HARDWARE.WPS is loaded into the document window.

Navigating the Works Document Window

Each document window includes controls (see Figure 2.7) that allow you to manipulate a document in a variety of ways. The mouse cursor, which is controlled by moving your mouse and pressing your mouse buttons, lets you select items and functions, as well as place the blinking text cursor anywhere in your document. The text cursor marks where the next text you type will appear.

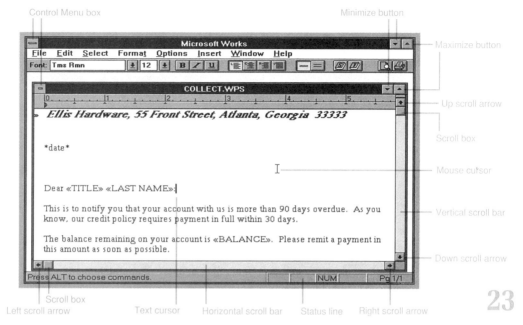

*Figure 2.7   Each document window features controls that
help you manipulate the window.*

Each document window also includes a *Control Menu box*,
Maximize and *Minimize* buttons, and *scroll bars.* Scroll bars let you
view hidden parts of a document and are covered in the next section,
"Viewing a Document." A window's Control Menu box is activated
by selecting on it with your mouse or by pressing Alt+hyphen on
your keyboard. The Control Menu allows you to change the size and
position of the window, as well as to close the document. These
functions are mainly for keyboard users. If you have a mouse (highly
recommended for any Windows user), Window controls can be used
instead of most of the Control Menu functions.

When you select the Maximize button, the document window
grows to its largest size, covering any other documents that may be
open (see Figure 2.8). When a document is maximized, the Maximize button changes to the *Restore* button (marked with two arrows),
which when selected, restores the window to its original size. When
you select the Minimize button, Works reduces the document
window to an icon, (see Figure 2.9) and places it at the bottom of the
Works desktop. To reopen the window, double-click on the icon, or
select Restore from the icon's Control Menu.

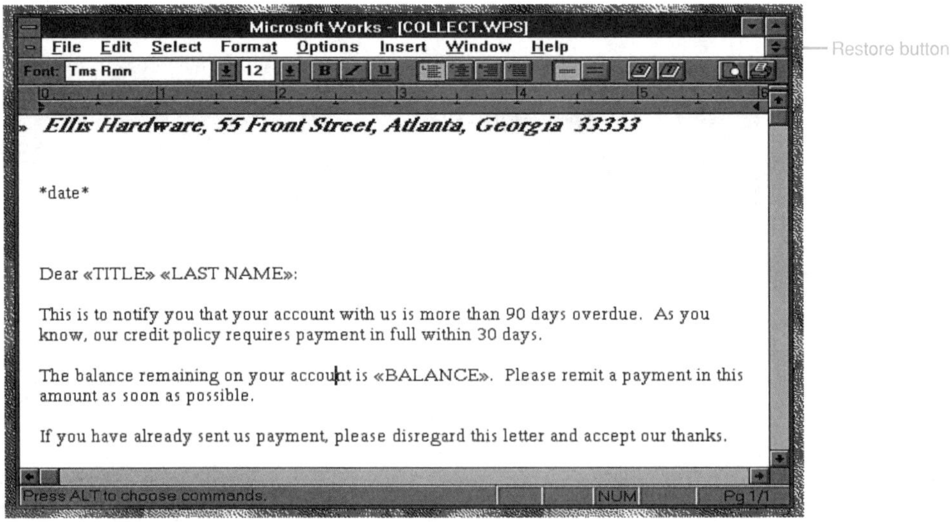

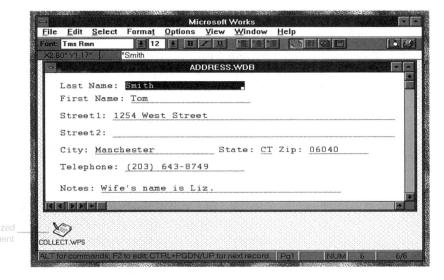

Restore button

Figure 2.8   *When a document is maximized, it covers the entire Works desktop.*

Minimized document

Figure 2.9   *A minimized document appears as an icon at the bottom of the Works desktop.*

24

The Works desktop also contains a *program* Control Menu box, which provides functions similar to those in a document's Control Menu. These functions, which allow you to manipulate the Works main window, are of interest mostly to keyboard users. However, if you use a mouse, you can exit Works quickly by double-clicking on the program Control Menu box. If you have no mouse, you can activate the program's Control Menu by pressing Alt+hyphen on your keyboard. When the menu appears, use the arrow keys to highlight the function you want, and press Enter to activate the function.

Viewing a Document

Many documents you'll create with Works will be too large to fit in the document window. You can use the window's controls, or your keyboard's arrow keys, to bring different sections of the document into view. For example, in HARDWARE.WPS, click on the window's down arrow, or press the down arrow key on your keyboard, to move down a line. Click on the up arrow, or your keyboard's up arrow key, to move up a line.

To move up or down an entire screen, click on the window's vertical scroll bar anywhere above or below the scroll box (see Figure 2.7). Pressing Page Up or Page Down on your keyboard has the same effect. If you want to move a great distance forward or backward through your document, use your mouse to drag the scroll box itself up or down in the scroll bar. The farther up or down you drag the scroll box, the farther up or down in the document you move.

There are many keyboard commands you can use to move through your document. For example, in a word processing document, you can quickly move the blinking text cursor to the beginning or end of a line, as well as word by word or paragraph by paragraph, by using special keystrokes. The keystrokes are listed in Table 2.1.

25

Table 2.1   The Cursor Movement Keystrokes.

Movement	Keystroke
Right one character	Right arrow
Left one character	Left arrow
Right one word	Ctrl+Right arrow
Left one word	Ctrl+Left arrow
Start of line	Home
End of line	End
Up one line	Up arrow
Down one line	Down arrow
Up one paragraph	Ctrl+Up arrow
Down one paragraph	Ctrl+Down arrow
Up one screen	PgUp
Down one screen	PgDn
Top of window	Ctrl+PgUp
Bottom of window	Ctrl+PgDn
Beginning of document	Ctrl+Home
End of document	Ctrl+End

Switching Between Windows

Works allows you to have several documents open simultaneously. Moreover, these documents need not be of the same type. You could, for example, have word processor, database, and spreadsheet documents open. Although you can have all these documents open at once, you can view and work with only one at a time.

The uppermost window (the one that covers any other open windows) is always the current document—that is, the document you can view or edit. To view or edit a different open document, you must switch to a new window. If part of the window is visible, you can click on it to bring it to the front. Usually though, the window you want will be hidden under other windows. To display a hidden window, select the window's name in the Window pull-down menu, as shown in Figure 2.10.

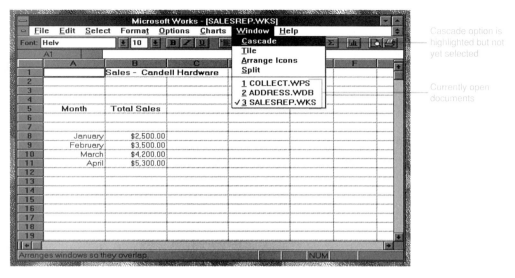

Figure 2.10   The Window menu shows all currently open documents, with a check next to the active document.

27

> **Note:** You can also select a window from the keyboard by pressing Alt+W, using your keyboard's arrow keys to highlight the desired window, and then pressing Enter. Other menu selections also can be made from the keyboard. Consult your Windows manual to learn about these standard keystrokes.

To see all hidden windows quickly, you can use the Cascade or Tile functions, found in the Window pull-down menu (see Figure 2.11 and Figure 2.12). Both functions allow you to see all open windows simultaneously, although you can only work with one at a time. To change the size of the desired window, select its Maximize button, or place your mouse cursor on one of the window's corners, hold down the left mouse button, and drag the corner to the desired size.

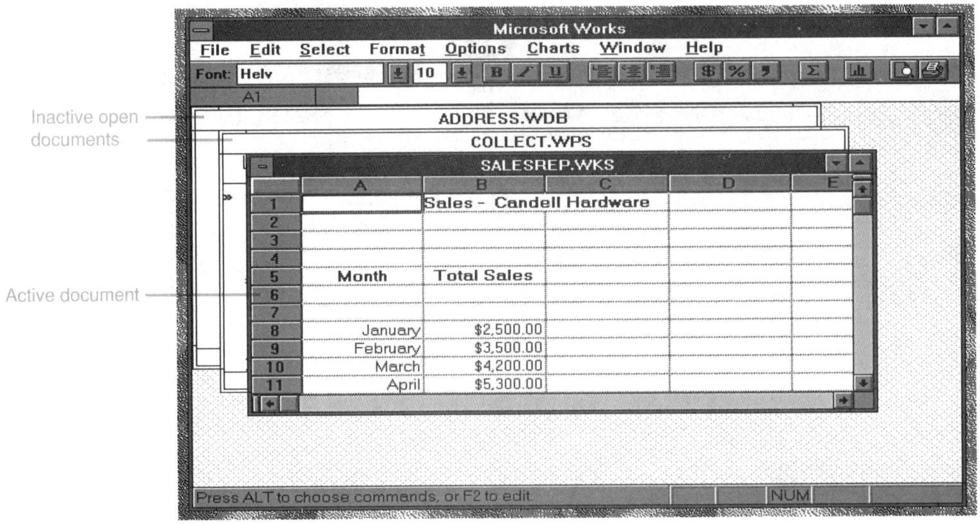

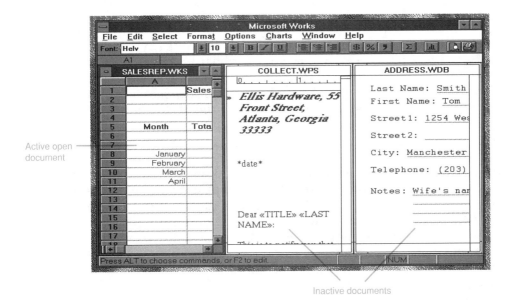

Figure 2.11   *Select Cascade from the Window pull-down menu to overlap all open windows.*

Figure 2.12   *Select Tile from the Window pull-down menu to arrange all open windows on the Works desktop.*

What You Have Learned

▶ To start a new file, select Create New File from the File pull-down menu.

▶ You should rename a new file as soon as you open it, by using the Save As function found on the File pull-down menu.

▶ You can close a document without exiting Works by selecting Close from the File pull-down menu.

▶ To save a file without closing it, select Save from the File pull-down menu.

▶ You can load a previously created file by selecting Open Existing File from the File pull-down menu.

▶ The Works document screen looks similar to other Windows application screens, and its commands and operations are accessed using the same methods.

▶ A document window's buttons and scroll bars let you see portions of a document that don't fit into the window.

▶ To switch to a new window, select the window's name in the Window pull-down menu.

29

Word Processor Basics

In This Chapter

▶ *Getting started*
▶ *Editing text*
▶ *Working with blocks of text*
▶ *Using Undo*
▶ *Searching and replacing text*
▶ *Showing special characters*

In this chapter you'll learn the basic operating procedures for using the Works word processor, including getting the word processor up and running on your computer, creating a new document, and editing an already created document. In addition, you'll learn about highlighting and working with text blocks, using the Undo function, using the Toolbar, using the Search and Replace function, and handling special characters. Readers experienced with word processing may want to skim this chapter for procedures specific to the Works for Windows word processor. If you've never used a word processor before, read this chapter carefully.

Starting the Word Processor

Before you can use the word processor, you must first start Works for Windows. The following Quick Steps detail the necessary steps for starting Works and the Works word processor.

 Starting the Word Processor

1. Double-click on the Microsoft Works icon shown in the Windows Program Manager. (Keyboard users should follow the start-up procedures outlined in Chapter 1.)

   Works for Windows loads and runs.

2. In the Startup dialog box, select the Word Processor button. (If the Welcome dialog box appears before the Startup box, select the Start Works Now button to make the Startup box appear.)

   The word processor screen appears. (See Figure 3.1.)

> **FYIdea:** By letting you use various fonts, font sizes, borders and graphics, the Works word processor is a lot like a small desktop publishing program. You can use it to save on printing bills by creating your own letterheads, flyers, and pamphlets.

Creating a New Document

Once you start the word processor, you automatically open a new document. The document has a default name of WORD1.WPS. Now start typing and your text appears in the document window. When

32

you reach the right margin of your document, the text automatically *wraps around* to the next line. You only need to press Enter at the end of a paragraph.

The blinking text cursor marks the current *insertion point,* the place where the next character will appear. Every time you type a character, the text cursor moves forward one space (see Figure 3.2). You can place the text cursor anywhere on the screen by clicking on the new location with your mouse, or by using the arrow keys on your keyboard.

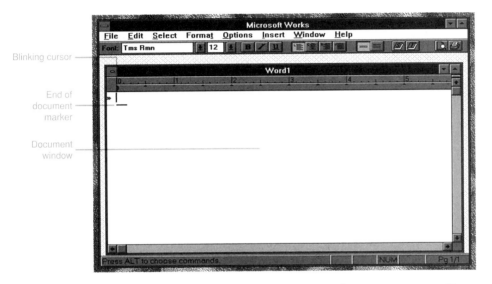

Blinking cursor —

End of
document —
marker

Document
window

33

Figure 3.1   *When the word processor first appears, you'll
be greeted with this screen.*

Editing Text

One wonderful thing about using a word processor is the ease with which you can edit a document. Making changes to your text is a snap, and best of all, doesn't require that you retype or change anything other than what you want to change. When you insert or delete words, sentences, paragraphs, and even whole pages, the word processor reformats everything automatically. When using a typewriter, inserting or deleting text usually means retyping an entire document. Not so with a word processor.

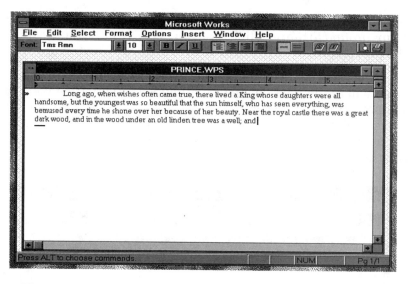

Figure 3.2   As you type, your text appears in the word processor's document window.

Inserting Text

Often when editing a document, you'll discover that you've left out a word or a sentence. You may even have new paragraphs or pages to add. Adding extra text usually means inserting it somewhere in the middle of your document. While this is a laborious procedure with a typewriter, it's easy with a word processor.

To add text to your document, simply move the text cursor to where you want to add the text. (Click on the location with the mouse or use your keyboard's arrow keys.) Then type the new text. As you type, the new characters push the old text to the right, making room for your inserted text.

Typing Over Text

A handy way to make corrections is to use the word processor's Overtype mode, where the characters you type replace the old characters in your document rather than pushing them to the right. This saves you from having to delete old characters before typing the new ones. There are two ways to select the Overtype mode:

▶ By pressing the Insert key on your keyboard.

▶ By selecting Overtype from the Options pull-down menu. (See Figure 3.3.)

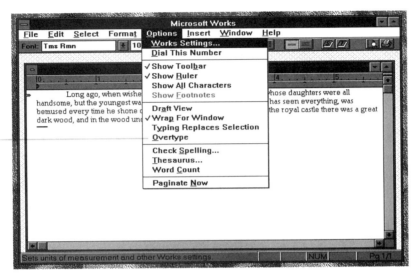

Figure 3.3   You can select Overtype mode from the Options pull-down menu.

Deleting Text

While correcting a document, you're likely to spot words or sentences that need to be removed from the text. Deleting small portions of your document is as easy as pressing the Backspace key, which moves the blinking text cursor to the left, deleting the character that was there. You can delete as many characters as you like this way.

You also can use the Delete key on your keyboard to remove characters from your text. Unlike the Backspace key, the Delete key removes characters to the right of the text cursor rather than to the left. When the character is deleted, the rest of your text automatically closes the gap.

If you have more than a few characters to delete, you'll probably want to take advantage of the word processor's block delete functions, described below.

Text Blocks

Sometimes it's quicker to edit a piece of text by first highlighting it as a *text block.* (See Figure 3.4.) When you highlight a text block, the next function you select will affect all of the text in the block. There are several ways to select a text block, depending upon the amount of text you want to include. Dragging your mouse pointer over a desired portion of text is one method that works for any amount of text.

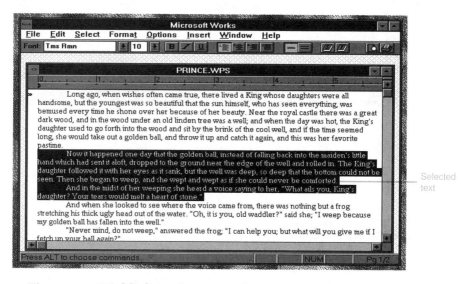

Figure 3.4   Highlighting lets you select large portions of text.

The following Quick Steps detail this procedure.

Highlighting Text

1. Place the mouse cursor to the left of the first character you want to highlight.

   The mouse cursor marks the beginning of the text block.

2. Press and hold down the left mouse button.

   The text cursor appears at the mouse cursor's location.

3. Still holding down the left mouse button, drag the mouse cursor over the text you want to highlight.

   Works highlights the text block.

4. Release the mouse button.

   The text block is ready to use.

In addition to selecting text with the mouse, there are many shortcut methods for highlighting different portions of text. Table 3.1 shows these shortcuts.

37

Table 3.1   Highlighting Shortcuts.

To highlight	Shortcut
A single word	Double-click on the word or move the text cursor over the word, and press F8 on your keyboard.
A line	Click next to the line in the left margin, or move the text cursor to the beginning of the line, and press Shift+End on your keyboard.
Several lines	Drag the mouse pointer up or down the left margin, or hold down the Shift key on your keyboard while pressing the up or down arrows.
A paragraph	Double-click to the left of the paragraph, or move the text cursor into the paragraph and press F8 four times.
An entire document	Hold down Ctrl on your keyboard and click in the document's left margin, or on your keyboard, press F8 five times.

Cutting and Pasting Text Blocks

In the course of revising a document, you'll undoubtedly find sentences, and even whole paragraphs, that need to be moved. The Works word processor allows you to cut blocks of text from your document and then paste them into a new location. To cut a block of text, first highlight the text. Then select Cut from the Edit pull-down menu (see Figure 3.5), or press Ctrl+X on your keyboard. Works removes the highlighted text from your document and stores it on Windows' *clipboard*. (The clipboard is a special place in memory where Windows stores cut and copied portions of a document.) To paste the block of text in its new location, place the blinking text cursor where you want the text, and then select Paste from the Edit pull-down menu (see Figure 3.5), or press Ctrl+V on your keyboard. Works inserts the contents of the clipboard into your document at the text cursor's location.

38

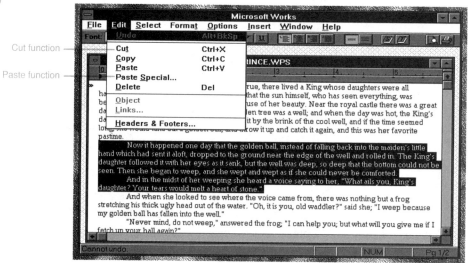

Cut function

Paste function

Figure 3.5   The Cut and Paste functions allow you to move around blocks of text.

The following Quick Steps summarize the cut and paste procedure.

Moving Text Blocks

1. Highlight the text you want to move.

   Works marks the text as selected.

2. Select Cut from the Edit pull-down menu, or press Ctrl+X on your keyboard.

   Works removes the highlighted text from your document.

3. Place the text cursor where you want the text moved, and then select Paste from the Edit pull-down menu, or press Ctrl+V on your keyboard.

   Works inserts the previously cut text into your document.

Note: Cut or copied text is stored in Windows' clipboard, where it remains until you cut or copy more text, or you exit Windows.

39

Warning: Deleted text (text that's been removed from your document by selecting Delete from the Edit menu, or by pressing the Delete key on your keyboard) is *not* copied into the clipboard. It can be restored only with the Undo function.

Undoing Your Last Action

Because many word processor functions are destructive—that is, they modify your document in ways that may not be easy to correct—Works lets you change your mind about certain actions. However, you must change your mind immediately after a function is performed. To undo a change, select Undo from the Edit pull-down menu, or press Alt+Backspace. The Undo function is especially handy when you accidentally delete a large chunk of text (see Figure 3.6).

Note that, when you pull down the Edit menu, Undo may be disabled (grayed out), as shown in Figure 3.7. This indicates that the option is inactive because the last function you performed is not reversible. For example, after you delete a block of text, the Undo function will be active, but after you restore the text using the Undo function, Undo will be inactive, indicating that you can't undo the undo.

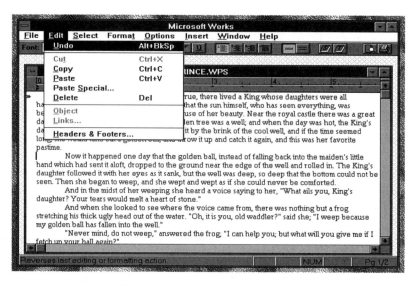

Figure 3.6   Undo lets you restore your document after an unwanted change.

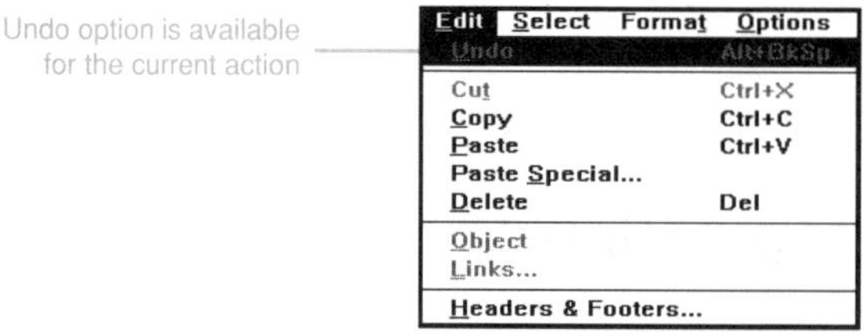

Undo option is available
for the current action

Figure 3.7   A grayed-out Undo command indicates that Undo is not available.

Search and Replace

The Search and Replace function is handy for making many corrections throughout your document. For example, you might want to use Search and Replace to change a name that you've misspelled in several places. When you invoke Search and Replace, Works examines your text for every occurrence of the "target" text and replaces it with the replacement text. To perform a search and replace, use your mouse or your keyboard's direction keys to position the text cursor at the beginning of the text you want to search for. Then, choose Replace from the Select pull-down menu. When the Replace dialog box appears, type the text for which you want to search. Press the Tab key on your keyboard, and then type the text that is to replace the target text. Press Enter or click on the dialog box's Replace button. Works then finds the first occurrence of the target text and asks whether you want it replaced. Select Yes to replace the text or No to leave it as is. Works continues to find all occurrences of the target text, until it reaches the end of the document or you cancel the function.

The following Quick Steps detail how to use Search and Replace.

 Searching and Replacing Text

1. Using your mouse or the keyboard arrow keys, position the blinking text cursor at the beginning of the text you want to search.

   The Search will begin from the text cursor's position and go through to the end of the document.

2. Choose Replace from the Select pull-down menu.

   The Replace dialog box appears (see Figure 3.8).

3. Type the text you want to search for.

   The text appears in the Find What text box.

4. Press the Tab key on your keyboard, and then type in the text that is to replace the old text.

   The replacement text appears in the Replace With text box.

41

5. Press Enter or select the Replace button in the Replace dialog box	Works finds the first occurrence of the target text and asks whether you want to replace it with the replacement text.
6. Select Yes to replace the text or No to leave the text as it is.	Works finds the next occurrence of the target text.
7. Repeat step 6 as often as necessary.	One by one, Works finds every occurrence of the target text.

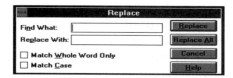

Figure 3.8   Search and Replace is a quick way to correct many occurrences of a text string.

There are several ways you can search for text. In fact, two buttons on the Search dialog box allow you to refine your search criteria somewhat. To limit the search to only complete words, select the Match Whole Word Only box. When you limit the search to whole words, Works will find only those occurrences of the target text bordered by spaces. For example, if you were searching for "the" with the Match Whole Word Only option on, Works would find only the word "the" and not every occurrence of the letters "the," such as found in the word "there." The Match Case button forces Works to search not only for the same letters, but also the same case. For example, with the Match Case option on, "Se" matches only "Se" and not "se."

Showing Special Characters

As you type a document, you place both visible and *invisible characters* in the text. Invisible characters include spaces, tabs, carriage returns and so on. Sometimes it's handy to be able to see these special characters in your text. You can do this by selecting

Show All Characters from the Options pull-down menu. When you select this option, a check mark appears in front of the option, letting you know it's on. To hide the special characters, select Show All Characters again. The check mark disappears, as do all the special characters in your document. (They're still there; you just can't see them.)

When the Show All Characters option is on, your screen looks something like Figure 3.9. The arrows are tabs, the little dots are spaces, and the characters that look like backwards P's are end-of-paragraph markers (carriage returns). The following list shows invisible characters and how they are entered into your text.

End-of-line (__): Press Enter while holding down Shift.

New paragraph (¶): Press Enter.

Space (···): Press the spacebar.

Tab (→): Press the Tab key.

This double space would be hard to catch without viewing special characters

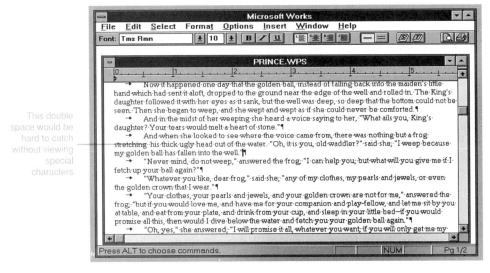

Figure 3.9   Sometimes it's handy to be able to see the special characters in your document.

What You Have Learned

▶ To start the Works word processor, you must first start Works from Windows Program Manager by double-clicking on its icon. You can then start the word processor by selecting the <u>W</u>ord Processor button in the Startup dialog box.

▶ Typing with a word processor is a lot like typing with a typewriter, except you only press Enter at the end of a paragraph.

▶ To insert text into your document, position the blinking text cursor at the insertion point and begin typing. Works automatically makes room for the new text as you type.

▶ To replace old text with new text, you can switch from the word processor's insert mode to Overtype mode.

▶ You can use your keyboard's Backspace and Delete keys to remove small portions of text.

▶ Highlighting text allows you to select a text block and treat it as a unit.

▶ By using the Cut and Paste functions, you can move blocks around in your document.

▶ The most recent change made to your document can usually be reversed by using the Undo function, which you select from the Edit pull-down menu.

▶ The Replace function lets you quickly make corrections throughout your document by finding a specific string of text and replacing it with a new one.

▶ As you type, you add both visible and invisible characters to your document. Invisible characters like carriage returns, spaces, and tabs, can be viewed by selecting Show A<u>l</u>l Characters from the Options pull-down menu.

Advanced Word Processing

In This Chapter

▶ *Selecting fonts and character sizes*
▶ *Using text attributes*
▶ *Creating indents*
▶ *Setting line and paragraph spacing*
▶ *Manipulating tabs*
▶ *Creating tables*
▶ *Inserting special characters*
▶ *Using the spell checker*
▶ *Using the thesaurus*
▶ *Creating footnotes*
▶ *Adding lines and borders*

Once you understand the basics of word processing, you're ready to tackle some of the sophisticated options that Works offers. The functions we'll cover in this chapter allow you to create more attractive and readable documents by giving you access to a host of formatting features, including different fonts, character styles, character sizes, and text alignments. You'll learn to make your documents look as professional as possible by using indents, line spacing, tab stops, tables, and borders. You'll also learn to use the thesaurus and spell checker.

Selecting Fonts

Several fonts are available for use in your documents. Which fonts are available depends on how your system is set up. In any case, you can select fonts in one of two ways:

► From the Menu bar
► From the Toolbar

Changing Fonts Using the Format Menu

To change fonts from the Menu bar, select Font & Style from the Format pull-down menu. The Font & Style dialog box appears (see Figure 4.1). Select the desired font in the Font list box, and then choose the OK button. The new font is applied to any new text you type.

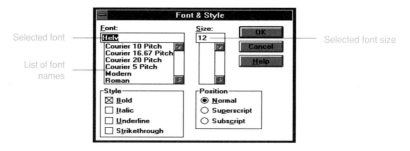

Figure 4.1   The Font & Style dialog box lets you change fonts, text sizes, and other text attributes.

You can change text you've already typed by highlighting it before choosing the font. The following Quick Steps summarize this combined procedure.

Changing the Font of Existing Text

1. Highlight the text you want to change.

   Works marks the text as selected.

2. Select Font & Style from the Format pull-down menu.

   The Font & Style dialog box appears.

3. Select the desired font in the Font list box.

Works highlights the selected font.

4. Click on the dialog box's OK button, or press Enter.

The new font is applied to the selected text block. ☐

Changing Fonts Using the Toolbar

Works' Toolbar also provides access to fonts (see Figure 4.2). To change a font from the Toolbar, click on the arrow next to the Font list box. The font list appears. Select the font you want. The chosen font then appears in the font text box and is applied to any new text you type.

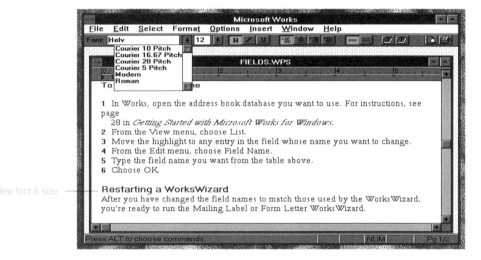

47

Figure 4.2 *The Toolbar lets you change fonts and font sizes quickly.*

> **Note:** The number of fonts available depends on the fonts installed into your Windows 3.0 system. To install or remove fonts, consult your Windows manual.

Selecting Character Sizes

Along with the font, the size of characters in a document determines how much text or data you can fit on a page. The smaller the text, the more you can fit. On the other hand, large font sizes are good for headlines and headings. It's easy to change character sizes using Works' Toolbar. As with fonts, you can change font sizes from the Menu bar or the Toolbar.

Changing Font Size Using the Format Menu

Changing font size from the Menu bar is similar to changing font type. Simply select Font & Style from the Format pull-down menu. The Font & Style dialog box appears. Select the desired size in the Size list box. Then click on the dialog box's OK button or press Enter. The new font size is used with any new text you type. As with fonts, you can change the size of already existing text by highlighting it before choosing the font size.

48

> **Note:** To print a document containing different character sizes and fonts, the character sizes and fonts must be available on your printer. For more information on printing documents with different fonts, consult your Windows manual.

Changing Font Size Using the Toolbar

To change font size from the Toolbar, click on the arrow to the left of the Points text box. The Points list box appears. Click on the font size you want. The chosen size appears in the Points text box, and the new size is applied to any new text you type, or to any text you have highlighted. See Figure 4.3 for an example of different font sizes.

> **Tip:** If the font size you want is not shown in the Points list box, you can change the size by typing the size you desire into the box. Keep in mind, though, that your printer may not support every font and font size that can appear on your screen.

Font size/
Points list box

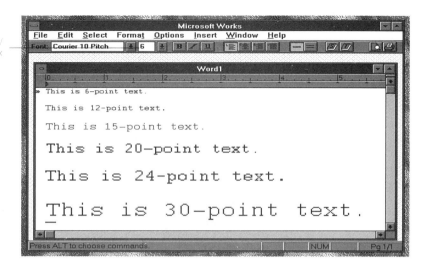

Figure 4.3   You can use many text sizes in a single document.

49

Bold, Italic, and Underlined Text

Many documents require special text attributes. For example, head-lines are usually printed in bold text, whereas book titles are underlined or italicized. Because Works is a *WYSIWYG* (What You See Is What You Get, pronounced "wizzy-wig") program, your text appears on the screen exactly as it does at printout time (unless you're viewing the document in draft mode, of course.)

To select bold, italic, or underlined text, you need only click on the B, I, or U button on the Toolbar, or press Ctrl+B, Ctrl+I, or Ctrl+U. Everything you type then appears with the selected at-tribute. You can even combine any or all of the attributes by clicking on more than one button. If you want to apply a text attribute to text you've already typed, highlight the text and click on the appropriate button. The highlighted text will take on the new attribute. To turn off an attribute, click on the button again.

The following Quick Steps detail this procedure.

 Changing the Text Attributes of Existing Text

1. Highlight the text you
   want to change.

   Works marks the text as
   selected.

2. Press Ctrl+B, Ctrl+I, or Ctrl+U, depending on whether you want bold, italic, or underlined text.	Works changes the highlighted text block to the newly selected attribute.
3. Repeat step 2 for each attribute you want to add.	Works adds each selected attribute to the highlighted text block. ☐

> **Tip:** You can also set a text attribute by bringing up the Font & Style dialog box, described in the previous sections. This is handy should you have the Toolbar turned off.

Text Alignment

You can align paragraphs in one of several ways:

- ▶ Left justified
- ▶ Centered
- ▶ Right justified
- ▶ Fully justified (meaning that the margins on both the left and right are of equal size).

Each alignment has special uses in your document. For example, you'd usually use left justification for the main text of a word processor document, whereas centered text is useful for subheads. To select an alignment, position your text cursor on the paragraph you want to align. To change more than one paragraph at once, highlight them. Then click on the L, C, R, or J button on the Toolbar, or press Ctrl+L, Ctrl+E, Ctrl+R, or Ctrl+J (see Figure 4.4). The selected paragraph immediately changes to the new format.

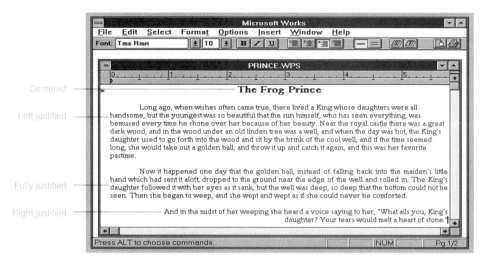

Figure 4.4   Works offers four types of paragraph alignment.

Indenting Paragraphs

Documents are more attractive and easier to read when they have properly set margins. Usually, you set the margins from the Page Setup & Margins dialog box, as described in Chapter 5. However, you can indent paragraphs beyond the regular margins by using the word processor's ruler, which Works displays at the top of each document window. When you indent a paragraph beyond the main margin, it stands off from the rest of the text (see Figure 4.5). Often this improves the readability of your document. You might, for example, want to indent a quotation or a list of instructions.

To indent a paragraph, first place the blinking text cursor anywhere on the paragraph you want to indent. Then, using your mouse pointer, drag the left-hand indent markers to the right (both the lower and upper marker). When you release the indent markers, the entire paragraph moves in to line up with the new setting. You also can indent the right side of any paragraph by dragging the right-hand indent marker to the left. To set indents from your keyboard, press Alt+T to select the Format menu, and then press A to bring up the Indents & Spacing dialog box, into which you can type the indents you require.

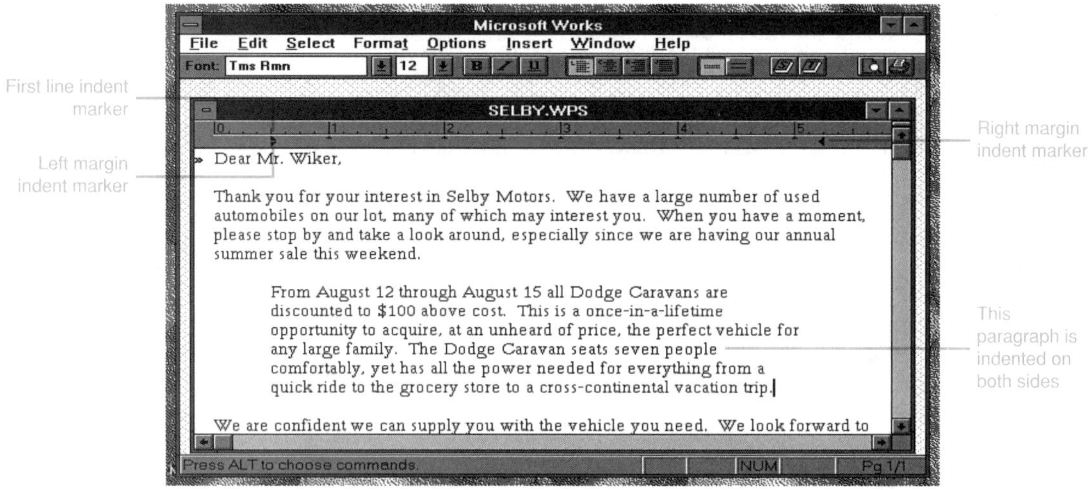

First line indent marker

Left margin indent marker

Right margin indent marker

This paragraph is indented on both sides

Figure 4.5 By indenting paragraphs, you can make them stand out from the rest of your text.

If you want to indent more than one paragraph, highlight the paragraphs before repositioning the indent markers. After you move the indent markers, Works indents all the highlighted paragraphs simultaneously.

> **Note:** Unlike margins, which are the same for every paragraph on every page, indents can be different from paragraph to paragraph.

First-Line Indenting

In most documents, you'll want to indent the first line of each paragraph. Although the Tab key works well for this purpose, you can have Works automatically do the indenting for you. You do this by setting the first-line indent marker. Then, each time you press Enter to end a paragraph, Works positions the blinking text cursor at the beginning of the next paragraph, at the position you should begin typing.

To set the first-line indent marker, place your mouse pointer on the upper marker of the left marker pair. Then press and hold the left mouse button and drag the marker to the right (only the top marker of the pair), to where you want the first-line indent set. Then release the mouse button. To set first-line indents from your keyboard, use the Indents & Spacing dialog box, as described earlier in the section on setting paragraph indents.

Line Spacing

The Works word processor offers variable line spacing for your documents, with the most popular—single and double—available right on the Toolbar. Usually, when you're writing a document, you'll want to stick to single-spacing so you can see as much of your work on the screen as possible. But often a finished document must be printed double-spaced. Changing to double-spacing is simple. Just highlight the text and click on the Toolbar's Double Space button.

53

Although single and double-spacing are most common, you can set your line spacing to any value you like by selecting Indents & Spacing from the Format pull-down menu. Use the following Quick Steps to change a section of text to another line-spacing setting.

 Changing Line Spacing to Any Value

1. Highlight the section of text you wish to space differently.	Works marks the highlighted text as a text block.
2. Select Indents & Spacing from the Format pull-down menu.	The Indents & Spacing dialog box appears, as shown in Figure 4.6.
3. Select the Space between lines text box and type the spacing value you require. For example, to get double-spacing, type **2**. To get triple-spacing, type **3**.	The number you type appears in the Space between lines text box.
4. Press Enter or click on the OK button.	The highlighted text changes to the new spacing setting.

> 🔦 **Tip:** You can use decimal numbers for your line spacing.
> A spacing value of 1.5, for example, is okay.

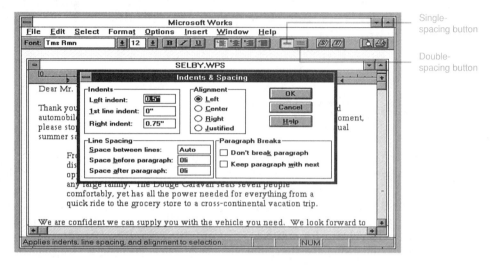

*Figure 4.6   The Indents & Spacing dialog box allows you
to change your document's line spacing, among other
things.*

You can set your line spacing before typing any text. Then any
new text you type uses the new line spacing setting. Like indenting,
line spacing can be different from paragraph to paragraph.

Paragraph Spacing

The Indents & Spacing dialog box also allows you to change the
amount of space between paragraphs. In most cases, you'll want to
keep your paragraphs spaced like the text—that is, one line for
single-spacing and two lines for double-spacing. If you want to
change the default paragraph spacing, however, you can do so by
changing the values in the Space before paragraph and Space after
paragraph text boxes in the Indents & Spacing dialog box. See Figure 4.7 for an example of paragraph spacing.

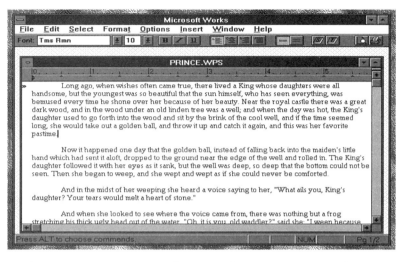

Figure 4.7   You can set the space between paragraphs to any value you like.

55

Setting and Removing Tabs

When you start a new document, Works automatically sets up default tabs on the document's ruler, one at each 1/2 inch mark. (They look like little upside-down T's.) You can move these tabs and even add new ones. To move a tab, place your mouse pointer on the tab, and then hold the left mouse button down while dragging the tab left or right. When you release the button, the tab stays in its new position. To add a new tab stop, place your mouse pointer on the ruler and click. The new tab appears where you clicked. To delete a tab you've added, use your mouse to drag the tab down off the ruler.

To set tabs from your keyboard, press Alt+T to activate the Format pull-down menu, and then press T to bring up the Tabs dialog box. Type the position of the new tab into the Position text box, and then press Enter. To delete a tab, highlight the tab setting in the Position text box, and then select the Delete button by pressing Alt+T.

While you can delete your own tabs, you can't directly delete Works' default tabs. You can, however, change their spacing. By changing their spacing to a large value, you can indirectly remove the default tab stops from the ruler. To change the spacing of the default tabs, use the following Quick Steps.

 Changing the Spacing of the Default Tabs

1. Select Tabs from the Format pull-down menu.

   The Tabs dialog box appears (see Figure 4.8).

2. Select the Default Tab Spacing text box.

3. Type a new value.

   The new setting appears in the Default Tab Spacing text box.

4. Click on the OK button or press Enter.

   The new default tabs appear on the ruler. □

> **Tip:** When you add a tab stop to the ruler, any default tab stops to the left of the new tab are removed.

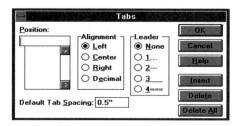

Figure 4.8   The Tabs dialog box lets you set many types of tabs.

The default tabs affect every paragraph in your text, whereas the tabs you add affect only the currently selected paragraphs. If you've highlighted no text before setting your own tabs, only the paragraph containing the text cursor is affected. In other words, if you want to add tabs that affect your entire document, you must first highlight all the text or choose All from the Select pull-down menu.

> **Tip:** If you don't need to see your tab settings, you can remove the ruler from the screen to provide more room for your text. To remove the ruler, select Show Ruler from the Options pull-down menu. To redisplay the ruler, select Show Ruler again.

Creating Tables

Using tabs, you can create all sorts of tables and lists, which allow you to present information in a more understandable way. To create a table, first set a tab stop for each column. Enter the table's text by pressing the Tab key on your keyboard, and then typing the text for the column. Press Tab again to get to the next column. When you get to the last column, press Enter to start a new line in your table. The tab stops from the previous line carry over into the next. Alternatively, you can press Shift+Enter at the end of a line, which groups the lines of the table into a single paragraph.

To help you organize information in your tables, you can select four types of tab stops:

▶ Left-aligned
▶ Centered
▶ Right-aligned
▶ Decimal

Left-aligned tabs are usually used for text entries, while centered tabs are good for column headings. Right-aligned or decimal tabs work well for numbers, with the latter aligning numbers according to their decimal points. Whenever you create a tab by clicking on the ruler, Works assumes you want a left-aligned tab, but using the procedure outlined in the following Quick Steps, you can create any type of tab.

 Setting Tab Alignments

1. Double-click on the tab whose alignment you want to change, or select Tabs from the Format pull-down menu.

   The Tabs dialog box appears.

2. In the Position list box, select the tab you want to change.

   Works highlights the chosen tab, which appears in the Position text box.

3. In the Alignment option box, select the type of alignment you want.

   Works highlights the selected option button.

4. Select the Insert button.   Works changes the selected tab's alignment.

5. Click on the OK button or press Enter.   Works removes the Tabs dialog box and returns you to your document.   ☐

Figure 4.9 shows an example of each kind of tab.

Tab markers

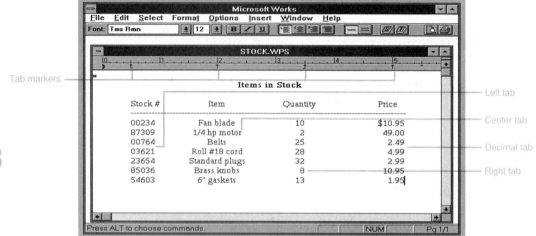

Left tab
Center tab
Decimal tab
Right tab

Figure 4.9   Tables help you organize information into a more readable form.

Besides setting tab alignment, you can use the Tabs dialog box to add *leaders* to your tables or lists. Leaders replace the spaces between columns, making it easier for the reader to follow the information from one column to the next. Leaders are commonly used in lists like tables of contents, as shown in Figure 4.10.

Use the following Quick Steps to add leaders to your tables or lists.

 Adding Leaders to Tabs

1. Double-click on the tab you want to edit, or select Tabs from the Format pull-down menu.   The Tabs dialog box appears.

58

2. In the Position list box, select the tab you want to change.

Works highlights the chosen tab, which appears in the Position text box.

3. In the Leader option box, select the type of leader you want.

Works highlights the selected option button.

4. Select the Insert button.

Works changes the selected tab's leader.

5. Click on the OK button or press Enter.

Works removes the Tabs dialog box and returns you to your document. ☐

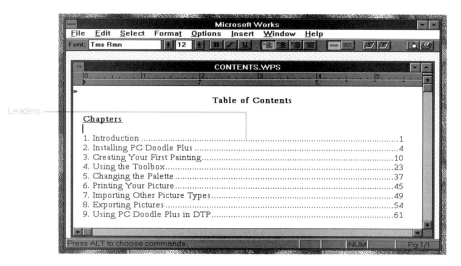

Figure 4.10   Leaders fill the spaces to the left of a tab with the selected character.

59

Note: Leaders fill the space to the left of the selected tab. If you want leaders between every column of a multi-column table, you must add leaders to each tab in the table.

Inserting Special Characters

Not every character in your document is a letter, a space, or punctuation. Some characters, such as tabs and paragraph markers, tell Works how to format your document or how to insert special text fields. We talked about some special characters in Chapter 3, but there are several other types you can insert into your documents. For example, you can have a document's file name or the current date automatically included somewhere in the text. Table 4.1 lists special characters you can add to your text.

Table 4.1   Special Characters.

Character	Function
Date	Prints the date in the short format
Filename	Prints the file name
Longdate	Prints the date in the long format
Time	Prints the time
-	Non-breaking hyphen (keeps hyphenated words from breaking at the end of a line)
-	Optional hyphen (adds hyphen to a word if it appears at the end of a line)
	Non-breaking space (keeps words together if they should fall at the end of a line)

Although the hard hyphen and the optional hyphen look the same, they function differently in your documents and are inserted in different ways.

The following Quick Steps detail how to insert special characters.

 Inserting Special Characters

1. In your text, position the text cursor where you want the special character placed.

The blinking text cursor marks the insertion point.

2. Select Special Character from the Insert pull-down menu.

The Special Character dialog box appears.

3. From the list in the dialog box, select the character you want to insert.

Works marks the character for insertion.

4. Press Enter or click on the OK button.

The special character appears at the insertion point.

> **Warning:** If you want to have accurate dates and times in your document, you must be sure that your system time and date are set correctly, because this is where Works gets this information. If you need to set your system time and date, consult your Windows manual.

Spell Checking a Document

When you're finished creating a document, you need to make sure it looks as professional as possible. And nothing makes a piece of writing look more unprofessional than misspelled words. Works' *spelling checker* helps you catch these mistakes. Even if you're a good speller, you should run your document through the spell checker, because it can help you find typographical errors that your proof-reading missed.

To start the spell checker, position the text cursor at the beginning of the text you want to check (usually at the beginning of your document). Then click on the Spell button on the Toolbar. (You can also start the spell checker by selecting Check Spelling from the Options pull-down menu.) When the spell checker finds a word not in Works' dictionary, the Spelling dialog box appears (see Figure 4.11).

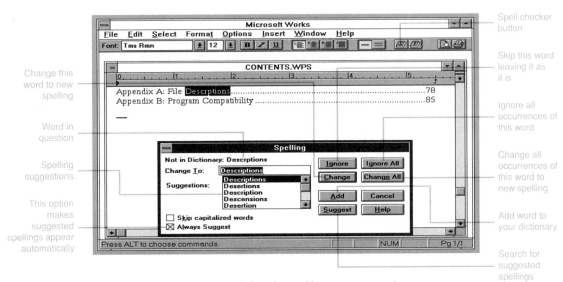

Figure 4.11 The spell checker offers many options.

62

There are several buttons in this dialog box. They are used as follows:

Ignore: Ignore the highlighted word one time.

Ignore All: Ignore every instance of the highlighted word.

Change: Change only this instance of the highlighted word to the word in the Change To text box.

Change All: Change every instance of the highlighted word to the word in the Change To text box.

Add: Add the highlighted word to the personal dictionary.

Suggest: Display a list of possible spellings.

Cancel: Discontinue the spell check.

Each time the spell checker finds a questionable word, you must select one of the above buttons. After you make your selection, the spell checker continues checking the rest of your document (unless you choose Cancel). The following Quick Steps detail the spell checking procedure.

 Spell Checking a Document

1. Position the text cursor at the beginning of the text you want to check.

   The blinking text cursor marks the location.

2. Click on the Spell button on the Toolbar, or select Check Spelling from the Options pull-down menu.

The spell checker starts, and the Spelling dialog box appears when Works finds a word not in its dictionary.

3. If you want to leave the word as it is, select the Ignore button.

Works ignores the highlighted word and then continues checking the document, bringing up the Spelling dialog box when it finds another word not in its dictionary.

4. If you want to add the highlighted word to your personal dictionary, select the Add button.

Works adds the word to the dictionary and then continues checking the document, bringing up the Spelling dialog box when it finds another word not in its dictionary.

63

5. If you want to see suggested spellings for the highlighted word, select the Suggest button.

Works searches its dictionary and displays suggested spellings in the Suggestions List box.

6. If you chose to view suggested spellings, select the proper spelling from the list (if the word you want isn't in the list, type the correctly spelled word into the Change To text box), and select the Change button.

Works replaces the highlighted word with the chosen spelling, and then continues checking the document, bringing up the Spelling dialog box when it finds another word not in its dictionary.

7. Repeat steps 3 through 6 until you reach the end of the document.

Works find all words not in its dictionary.

□

> **FYIdea:** If you add to your personal dictionary the names of people and places that appear frequently in your documents, Works will automatically ignore them during a spell check, rather than flagging them as misspelled words.

> **Tip:** While a spell checker can find misspelled words, it can't tell you if you've used the wrong word. For example, a spell checker can't tell, as far as usage goes, the difference between to, too, and two.

Using the Thesaurus

Sometimes, when writing, you need to replace a word in your document with one that's more precise. Works' built-in thesaurus can help by suggesting synonyms. The following Quick Steps detail how to use the Thesaurus.

Q Finding Synonyms

1. Position the blinking text cursor on the word for which you want a synonym, and click on the Thesaurus button on the Toolbar (or select Thesaurus from the Options menu.)

    The Thesaurus dialog box appears, as shown in Figure 4.12.

2. Select the correct meaning in the Meanings list box.

    Works displays possible synonyms in the Synonyms list box.

3. If none of the meanings in the Meanings list box is quite right, select the one closest in meaning, and then choose the Suggest button.

    A new list of meanings appears.

4. Choose a synonym from the list in the Synonyms list box.

    Works highlights the selected word.

5. Select the Change button.

    Works replaces the selected word in the document with the chosen synonym. ☐

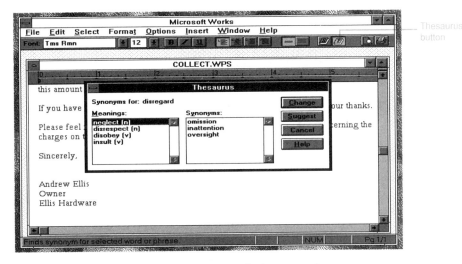

Figure 4.12   *Works' thesaurus can help you spice up your writing.*

Headers and Footers

Using *headers* and *footers,* you can add page numbers, titles, dates, and any other text, to the top and bottom of each page of a document. (Headers appear on the top and footers on the bottom.) In a multi-page document, you'll at least want to have a header or footer containing the page number. Because headers and footers can include many types of information, you must use special codes to tell Works what to print and where to print it. The codes are listed in Table 4.2.

Table 4.2   *Special Codes for Headers and Footers.*

Code	Function
&l	Align the following characters to the left
&r	Align the following characters to the right
&c	Center the following characters
&p	Print the page number

continues

Table 4.2   continued

Code	Function
&f	Print the file name
&d	Print the date in short format (for example, 01/21/91)
&n	Print the date in long format (for example, January 21, 1991)
&t	Print the time
&&	Print an ampersand

The above codes may seem cryptic at first, but it's actually easy to use them to create all types of headers and footers. For example, to create the header shown in Figure 4.13, you'd type

```
&lThe Frog Prince&rPage &p
```

Just about any combination of codes and text can be combined in a header or footer.

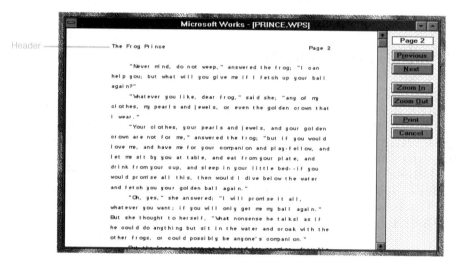

Figure 4.13   Headers and footers let you add helpful information to the top or bottom of every page.

To add a header or footer, first select <u>H</u>eaders & Footers from the Edit menu. The Header & Footers dialog box appears. This dialog box contains text boxes into which you can enter your header and footer, as well as several options that control the way your headers and footers are displayed. When the dialog box appears, if the Use

Header and Footer Paragraphs box is checked, turn it off, setting Works to create standard headers and footers. If you don't want a header or footer on your document's first page, select the No Header on 1st Page and No Footer on 1st Page check boxes. Type your header or footer in the Header or Footer text box. Then press Enter or click on the OK button. This procedure is outlined in the following Quick Steps.

 Adding Headers and Footers

1. Select Headers & Footers from the Edit menu.

   The Header & Footers dialog box appears.

2. If the Use Header and footer paragraphs box is checked, turn it off.

   Works is set to create standard headers and footers.

3. If you want no header or footer on your document's first page, select the No header on 1st page and No footer on 1st page check boxes.

   If you select these boxes, Works will print headers and footers starting on page 2 of your document.

4. Type your header or footer in the Header or Footer text box. Then press Enter or click on the OK button.

   Works adds the header or footer (or both) to your document.

> **Note:** You can't see a header or footer in your document unless you're in print preview. However, your headers and footers will appear on your pages at print time.

> **Tip:** If you want to check or edit your headers and footers, just select Headers & Footers from the Edit menu to bring up the Headers & Footers dialog box.

67

Creating Footnotes

Many types of documents require that you list information sources in footnotes at the bottom of a page. You also can use footnotes to include interesting side notes in a document, notes that you don't want to place in the main text. The footnote option is located in the Insert menu. When you select it, a reference number is inserted at your text cursor, and the Footnote dialog box appears. You can choose to reference the footnote with a character, such as an asterisk (*), or a number. Once you make this choice, you can type in your footnote in the window pane that appears. The following Quick Steps outline this procedure.

 Creating a Footnote

1. Move the blinking text cursor to where you want the footnote reference mark.

   When the footnote is created, Works will place the reference number at the chosen location.

2. Select Footnote from the Insert pull-down menu.

   The Footnote dialog box appears.

3. Select the Numbered or Character mark option button.

   Works marks the selected button.

4. If you chose the Character Mark option, enter the desired character in the Mark text box.

   When the footnote is created, Works adds the character to the footnote.

5. Click on the OK button or press Enter.

   A footnote pane appears at the bottom of the document window (see Figure 4.14).

6. Type the footnote text.

   The footnote text appears in the footnote pane.

7. When finished typing the footnote text, place the mouse pointer over the narrow bar separating the text and footnote panes, and double-click (or select Show Footnotes from the Options menu).

   Works removes the footnote pane from the screen.

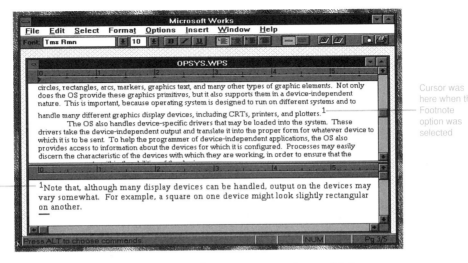

Figure 4.14   Works creates footnote panes into which you can type footnote text.

You can view your footnotes at any time by selecting Show Footnotes from the Options pull-down menu. To edit a footnote, first bring up the footnote pane, and then press F6. The blinking text cursor appears in the pane, allowing you to edit the footnote text. To delete a footnote, highlight the footnote's reference marker and press Delete on your keyboard. Works removes the selected footnote, and if necessary, renumbers succeeding footnote entries.

Creating Lines and Borders

Although the Works word processor is far from a desktop publishing program, it does allow you to add borders and lines to your documents.

FYIdea: Use these graphic elements to enhance the focus and readability of your documents. You might, for example, want to put a box around a list or a chart to separate it from the text and draw the reader's attention to it.

Works offers three types of borders:

- ▶ Single line
- ▶ Double line
- ▶ Bold

In addition, you can choose a full border (a box) or any combination of lines on the right, left, top, and bottom of the selected text. The following Quick Steps illustrate how to add lines and borders to your document.

 Adding Lines and Borders

1. Highlight the paragraph or paragraphs around which you want the border.

   Works marks the paragraphs as a text block.

2. Select Border from the Format pull-down menu.

   The Border dialog box appears, as shown in Figure 4.15.

3. In the Border option box, select the lines you want to add.

   Works highlights the selected option buttons.

4. In the Line Style option box, select the border style you want.

   Works highlights the selected option button.

5. Click on the OK button or press Enter on your keyboard.

   Works adds the selected border to your document.

Tip: If you want a border around a single paragraph, you don't need to highlight the paragraph. Just place the text cursor somewhere in the paragraph, and then create the border.

To remove a line or border, highlight the paragraph, select Border from the Format pull-down menu, and deselect the lines in the Border option box. (Click on any highlighted button.)

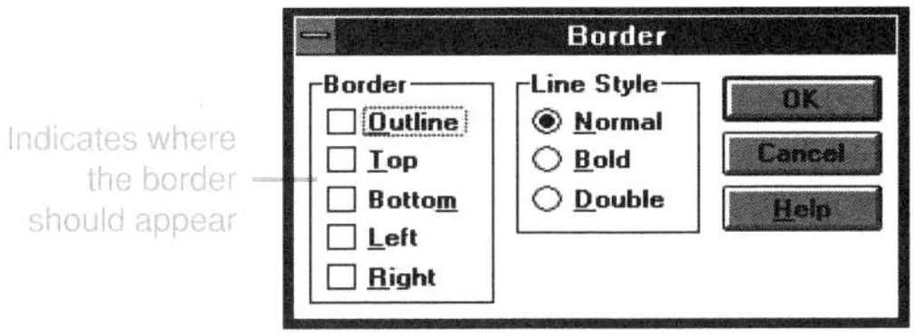

Figure 4.15   The Border dialog box offers different types of lines and borders.

What You Have Learned

▶ You can use many fonts, font sizes and font attributes in your documents.

▶ The Toolbar offers four types of text alignment: left justified, centered, right justified, and fully justified.

▶ The word processor's ruler lets you set left and right indents for individual paragraphs.

▶ Using the Indents & Spacing dialog box, you can adjust line and paragraph spacing to any value you want.

▶ Besides setting indents, the ruler allows you to add or move tab stops.

▶ You can create well-organized tables by using tabs and tab alignments.

▶ By inserting special characters into your text, you can print file names, dates, times, and other information.

▶ The spell checker finds misspelled words in your document.

▶ The thesaurus helps you find synonyms for weak words.

▶ To add headers or footers to your document, select Headers & Footers from the Edit pull-down menu.

▶ To create a footnote, select Footnote from the Insert pull-down menu.

▶ You can add various types of lines and borders to your documents by selecting Border from the Format pull-down menu.

▶ For quick access to many options described in this chapter, click on the appropriate buttons on the Toolbar.

71

Printing

In This Chapter

- ▶ *Changing page setup and margins*
- ▶ *Using print preview*
- ▶ *Printing a document*

After you've created a document, you'll want to print one or more hard copies. Getting a document to print exactly the way you expect requires some experimentation, especially if you're inexperienced with printers and word processors. Luckily, Works boasts several functions that help you get a document printed right the first time. In this chapter, we'll look at these functions, including setting margins, changing your page setup, using print preview, and sending a document to a printer.

Page Setup and Margins

When you open a new document, Works automatically creates the page setup, including default margins, paper length and width, and first page number. For most documents, these settings work fine.

However, you can change any of the settings at any time. To change your page setup, select Page Setup & Margins from the File pull-down menu. The Page Setup & Margins dialog box appears (see Figure 5.1). To change a setting, select the appropriate text box and type a new value. Then press Enter or click on the OK button.

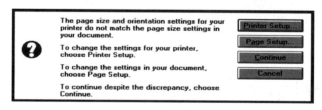

Figure 5.1   *The Page Setup & Margins dialog box lets you customize your page settings.*

The Top margin, Bottom margin, Left margin, and Right margin text boxes are self-explanatory. They control the amount of white space around the edges of your document. The Header margin text box sets the amount of space between the top of the page and your headers. The Footer margin text box sets the amount of space between the bottom of the page and your footers.

For most documents, you should leave the Page length and Page Width text boxes set at their default values of 11" and 8 1/2". However, if you're using a different paper size, you need to set the paper size in these boxes. Be aware that your page length and width settings should match those in your printer setup. Otherwise, when you try to print your document, you'll get the warning shown in Figure 5.2. Printer setup is accessible by selecting Printer Setup from the File pull-down menu.

Figure 5.2   *If your page and printer settings don't match, Windows sends you a warning.*

> **Tip:** If you need help setting up or modifying your printer configuration, printer installation and settings are explained in your Windows manual.

The 1st page number text box controls the number assigned to the first page of your document. In most cases, it should stay set to its default value of 1. However, if you want to begin numbering at a different value, type the first page number in this box. Each page in your document is numbered consecutively, starting with this value.

Print Preview

Before you print a document, use print preview to see how the printed copy will look. Previewing your document can save you time and paper, because you will then avoid printing documents that are not formatted the way you think they are. In print preview, you can see headers, footers, footnotes, margins, line spacing, and more, all as they will appear in your final document.

To start Print preview, select Print Preview from the File pull-down menu or click on the Toolbar's Print preview button. The print preview screen then appears, showing a page of your document (see Figure 5.3). Several buttons on this screen allow you to manipulate the page image in different ways. These buttons are described in Table 5.1.

Table 5.1   Print Preview Button Functions.

Button	Function
Previous	Moves to the previous page
Next	Moves to the next page
Zoom In	Magnifies the page image
Zoom Out	Reverses the page magnification
Print	Prints the document
Cancel	Returns to the document window

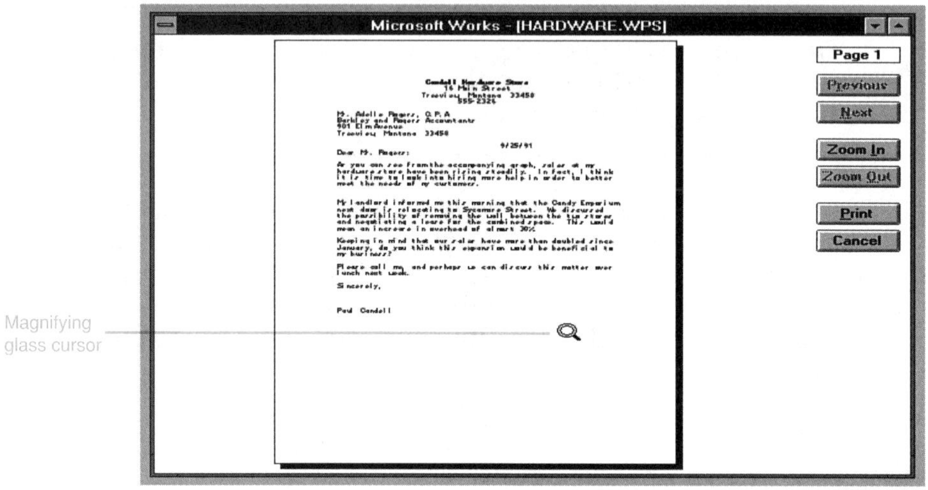

Magnifying
glass cursor

*Figure 5.3   Print preview lets you see your document in
the format in which it will be printed.*

> **Tip:** When you move your mouse cursor over the preview
> page, the text cursor changes to a *magnifying glass.* By
> clicking on the magnifying glass on the page, you can activate
> the page magnification feature without selecting the Zoom
> buttons. By double-clicking on the page, you can jump from no
> magnification to full magnification (or back again) in one step.

Printing a Document

When you're finished formatting your document, you'll want to
print a copy. To print a document, select Print from the File pull-
down menu or click on the Tool box's Print button. The Print dialog
box appears (see Figure 5.4). If you like, you can change the number
of copies to print by selecting the Number of Copies box in the Print
dialog box, and changing the number. You also can choose to print
the document in "draft" form, by selecting the Draft Quality Printing
box. (A document printed in draft form contains no graphic elements, such as bold, italic, or underline, charts or graphs, and so on.

Only the text itself is printed, which significantly speeds the printing process.) Finally, when printing a multipage document, you can select exactly which pages to print by typing the starting and ending page numbers into the From and To boxes. When you're ready to start the printing process, press Enter or select the Print dialog box's OK button.

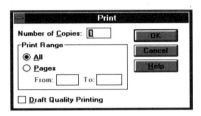

Figure 5.4   The Print dialog box allows you to customize the printing process.

The following Quick Steps outline the procedure for previewing and printing a document.

Previewing and Printing a Document

1. Select Print Preview from the File pull-down menu, or click on the Toolbar's Print preview button.	The Print preview screen appears.
2. Check the page image to be sure it's formatted correctly. If you need to make changes, select the Cancel button.	If you select the Cancel button, Works returns to your document window, where you can do the required editing.
3. If the page image looks okay, select the Print button.	The Print dialog box appears.
4. If required, change the number of copies to print by selecting the Number of Copies box and changing the number.	When you print your document, Works will print the number of copies you select.

5. If you want only a draft copy of your document, select the Draft Quality Printing box.	Works marks the option as selected.
6. If necessary, select which pages to print by typing the starting and ending page numbers into the From and To boxes.	Works will print only those pages you select.
7. Press Enter or click on the OK button.	Works prints your document.

> **FYIdea:** Whenever you print an important letter, be sure to print a copy for your records, by entering "2" into the Number of Copies text box of the Print dialog box.

What You Have Learned

▶ You can change a document's page setup, margins, and starting page number by selecting Page Setup & Margins from the File pull-down menu.

▶ Your page setup and printer setup should match, or you'll get a warning from Windows.

▶ Print preview allows you to see how your document will look when printed.

▶ To print a document, you can either click on the Toolbar's Print button or select Print from the File pull-down menu.

Microsoft Draw

In This Chapter

- ▶ *Getting started*
- ▶ *Using the drawing tools*
- ▶ *Framing and filling objects*
- ▶ *Aligning objects to the grid*
- ▶ *Editing and working with objects*
- ▶ *Choosing patterns and lines*
- ▶ *Importing pictures*
- ▶ *Pasting a drawing into a document*

Microsoft Draw is a full-featured drawing program that allows you to add sophisticated graphic objects to your word processor documents. Unlike traditional paint programs, which treat the entire picture as a single object, Microsoft Draw creates drawings by combining smaller objects, such as lines, squares, circles, and even freehand-drawn images. If you've used only paint programs before, Microsoft Draw will take some getting used to. In this chapter, we'll show you everything you need to know to create your own drawings.

Starting a Drawing

While you can start the word processor, database, or spreadsheet programs from the works startup screen, Microsoft Draw can be started only from within the word processor. To start a drawing from within a word processor document, place the blinking text cursor in the position you want the drawing, and then select Drawing from the Insert pull-down menu. After a few seconds, the Microsoft Draw main screen appears, as shown in Figure 6.1.

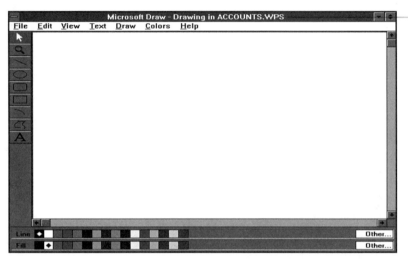

Current word processing document

Figure 6.1   Microsoft Draw can be started only from within the Works word processor.

Once Microsoft Draw appears on your screen, you can start your drawing by selecting buttons from the Tool box and creating shapes in the drawing window.

The Drawing Tools

On the left side of the Microsoft Draw screen are nine tool buttons, which you use to select the various drawing functions. Each button in the Tool box is marked with an icon that reminds you of that button's function. For example, to draw a rectangle, you select the button marked with the rectangle icon (see Figure 6.2). Following is a list of the tools and descriptions of how each is used.

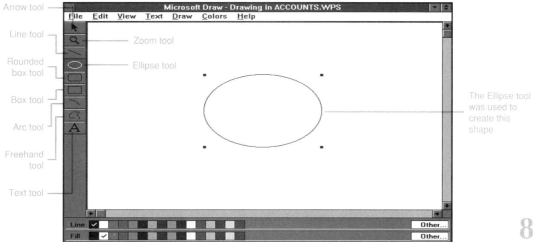

Figure 6.2   After selecting a tool, hold down the left mouse button while dragging the pointer to create your shape.

81

Arrow: Use the Arrow tool to select, change, or move objects. After selecting the Arrow button, place the mouse pointer over the object you want to select and click on it. When you select an object, its four handles appear. By placing your mouse pointer on a handle, holding down the left button, and dragging the handle, you can change the size and shape of an object. To move a selected object, place the arrow over the object and hold down the left mouse button. When you move the pointer, the object follows. Release the button to drop the object in its new location.

You can also use the arrow to select several objects at once by placing the arrow on the drawing's background, holding down the left button, and dragging the pointer across the screen. A dotted frame follows the mouse pointer. When you release the mouse button, Works selects all objects inside the frame.

Zoom: Use the Zoom tool to magnify or reduce a portion of your drawing. Select the Zoom button, and then move the mouse pointer over the drawing window. The mouse pointer changes to a magnifying glass. Click anywhere to magnify that portion of the screen. To reduce the size of the image, hold down the Shift key when you click. You can also zoom by selecting an entry from the View pull-down menu.

Line: Use the Line tool to draw straight lines. After selecting the Line button, place your mouse cursor on the drawing and hold down the left mouse button. This marks the beginning of your line. Next, still holding down the mouse button, drag the pointer to the line's end point, then release the mouse button. Works draws a line between the two points. To draw a line from its center, hold down the Ctrl key while dragging the mouse pointer. If you want to force a line to 45 degree increments, hold down the Shift key while dragging the mouse pointer.

Ellipse: Use the Ellipse tool to draw ovals and circles (see Figure 6.3). First, select the Ellipse button, and then move the mouse pointer to where you want the oval or circle. Hold down the left mouse button and drag the pointer across the screen. A dotted-line shape expands or contracts with the mouse's movement. When you have the shape you want, release the mouse button. If you want to draw a perfect circle, hold down the Shift key while dragging the mouse pointer. If you want to draw an oval or circle from the center, hold down the Ctrl key (along with the Shift key for a perfect circle).

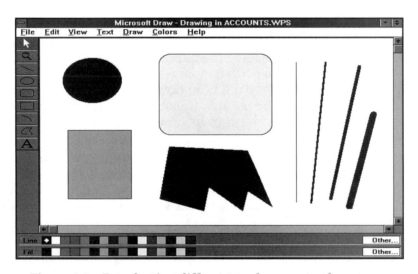

Figure 6.3   By selecting different tools, you can draw many types of objects.

Rounded Box: Use the Rounded Box tool to draw rectangles and squares with rounded corners. Select the Rounded Box button. Then move the mouse pointer to your drawing, hold down the left mouse button, and drag the pointer across the screen. A dotted-line shape expands or contracts with the mouse's movement. When you have the shape you want, release the mouse button. If you want to draw a perfect square (with rounded corners), hold down the Shift key while dragging the mouse pointer. If you want to draw a rectangle or square from the center, hold down the Ctrl key (along with the Shift key for a perfect square).

Box: Use the Box tool to draw rectangles and squares with squared corners. Select the Box button, and then move the mouse pointer to your drawing. Hold down the left mouse button and, while drag the pointer across the screen. A dotted-line shape expands or contracts with the mouse's movement. Release the mouse button when you have the shape you want. If you want to draw a perfect square, hold down the Shift key while dragging the mouse pointer. If you want to draw a rectangle or square from the center, hold down the Ctrl key (along with the Shift key for a perfect square).

83

Arc: Use the Arc tool to draw partial ovals and circles. Select the Arc button, move your mouse pointer to your drawing, and, while holding down the left mouse button, drag the mouse pointer across the screen. Release the mouse button when you have the shape you want. To draw a portion of a perfect circle, hold down the Shift key while dragging the pointer. To draw an arc from its center point, hold down the Ctrl key (along with the Shift key for a portion of a perfect circle).

Freehand: Use the Freehand tool to draw a series of connected straight lines or freehand objects. Select the tool, and then click on where you want to begin drawing. Drag the mouse pointer (without holding down the left button) and the line follows. Click to end the line and start another. To draw freehand, hold down the left mouse button while dragging the pointer. You can end a freehand or line drawing by double-clicking, or by bringing a line near your starting point and clicking once. In the latter case, Works automatically connects your last line to the starting point.

A   *Text:* Use the Text tool to add labels, notes, and other text objects to your drawings. Select the Text tool. Then move the mouse pointer to your drawing and click. A blinking text cursor appears. Type your text and press Enter. The text is marked as a single object, which you can position wherever you like. You can modify the text object in many ways, both with the regular object functions and by using the functions available in the Text pull-down menu, which include bold, italic, and underlined text.

Framed and Filled Objects

Most objects that you create with Microsoft Draw are actually made up of two parts: a *frame* and a *fill.* The frame is the line around the object's perimeter, and the fill is the color that fills the interior of the object. When you create an object, you can choose to have either the frame or the fill turned off. You'd probably never want to turn both off, though, since you would then create a phantom object that, although it exists on your screen, cannot be manipulated.

Objects made up of only a frame are *hollow.* That is, when you place the object on top of another, it acts like a window, allowing you to see through it to the object beneath. A hollow object can be manipulated only by its frame. An object with a fill, even if the fill is the same color as the background, is said to be *solid.* When you place this type of object on top of another, it blocks the lower object from view. Figure 6.4 shows a hollow and a solid object.

You can turn off the frame or fill attributes, either before or after you create an object, by selecting Framed or Filled from the Draw pull-down menu. To turn off the frame or fill of an already existing object, select the object before selecting Framed or Filled attributes in the Draw menu.

You can also control the colors assigned to your objects' frames and fills. To set the frame color, select the chosen color in the Line palette, shown at the bottom of the screen. To change the fill color, select a new color in the Fill palette, which is located right below the Line palette. You can set the colors before or after creating an object. To change an already existing object's colors, select the object before changing the palette.

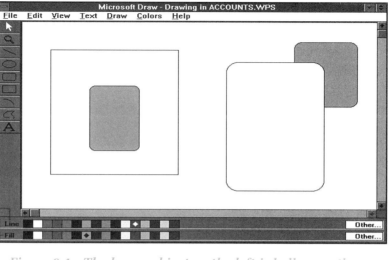

Figure 6.4 The larger object on the left is hollow, so the smaller object shows through. The larger object on the right is solid, so it blocks out objects over which it is placed.

85

Note: Active menu entries and other options may be marked by either a diamond or a checkmark. Works uses diamonds when the marked options will be used for the next object created. Works uses checkmarks to show which attributes are assigned to a selected object.

Snap to Grid

To help you line up objects more precisely, Microsoft Draw uses a *hidden* grid. You can take advantage of this grid by turning on the Snap to Grid function, found in the Draw pull-down menu. When this option is on, objects automatically "snap" (align themselves) to the nearest grid line. To see how this works, create a square, turn on the Snap to Grid function, and then move the square around the screen. As you drag the square, it jumps from one grid alignment to the next. Now, turn off the Snap to Grid function and move the square again. This time it moves smoothly around the screen; you can place it anywhere. Figure 6.5 illustrates objects lined up with the Snap to Grid function on.

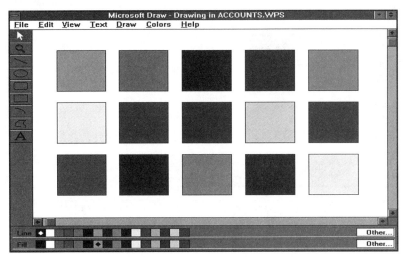

Figure 6.5   Using the Snap to Grid function, you can easily align many objects.

Cutting, Deleting, Copying, and Pasting Objects

Because your drawing comprises many separate objects, you can edit the objects almost as you would words in a word processor. You can make copies of objects and then paste them to different areas of the screen. You can delete objects or move them to new locations. You can rearrange and manipulate objects just about any way you like.

The cutting and copying functions are similar in that both move the selected object into a storage area known as the *clipboard* (see Figure 6.6). (To learn more about the clipboard, consult your Windows manual.)

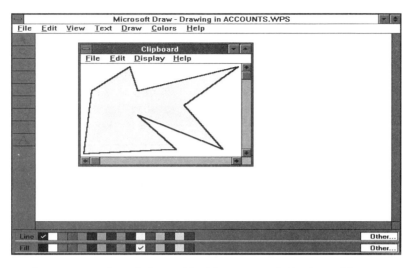

Figure 6.6   The clipboard holds a copy of the last object that was cut or copied.

 Tip: The difference between cutting and copying is that, when you cut an object, you both copy it to the clipboard and remove it from the screen, whereas when you copy an object, you copy it into the clipboard without removing it from the screen.

To cut or copy an object, first select the object. Then select Cut or Copy from the Edit pull-down menu.

When you cut or copy an object, it moves onto the clipboard, from which you can paste the object anywhere you like. Once the object is on the clipboard, you can paste it not only into your drawing, but also directly into any program that supports the clipboard and that accepts graphic images from Microsoft Draw. The Quick Steps below review how to copy an object and then paste it into your drawing.

Copying and Pasting an Object

1. Click on the object you want to copy.

Works marks the object as selected.

2. Select Copy from the Edit pull-down menu.	Works copies the object onto the clipboard.
3. Select Paste from the Edit pull-down menu.	A copy of the object appears on the screen.
4. Drag the object to its new location.	When you release the mouse button, the object stays in position. ☐

> **Tip:** Once you've copied or cut an object, you can paste as many copies of the object as you like by repeatedly selecting Paste from the Edit pull-down menu.

When you delete an object, you remove it from the screen without copying it onto the clipboard. In other words, a deleted object is gone forever (unless you immediately select Undo from the Edit menu). To delete an object, select it with your mouse, and then select Clear from the Edit pull-down menu or press the Delete key on your keyboard.

> **FYIdea:** You can enhance your work with reusable icons, such as this one, by saving the icon into its own word processing file. Then, copy it out of that document and paste it wherever you need it in future documents. Name the document by the same name you choose for your icon.

Selecting Patterns and Line Styles

Until now, we've talked only about solid fills. But Microsoft Draw actually offers seven different fill patterns that you can use to add texture and variety to the objects that make up your drawing. You can select a fill pattern before or after you create an object. To choose a fill pattern, select Pattern from the Draw pull-down menu. The Pattern menu appears, as shown in Figure 6.7. Choose the pattern you want. Works marks the pattern as selected and removes the menus from the screen. To change the fill pattern of an already existing object, select the object before choosing the pattern.

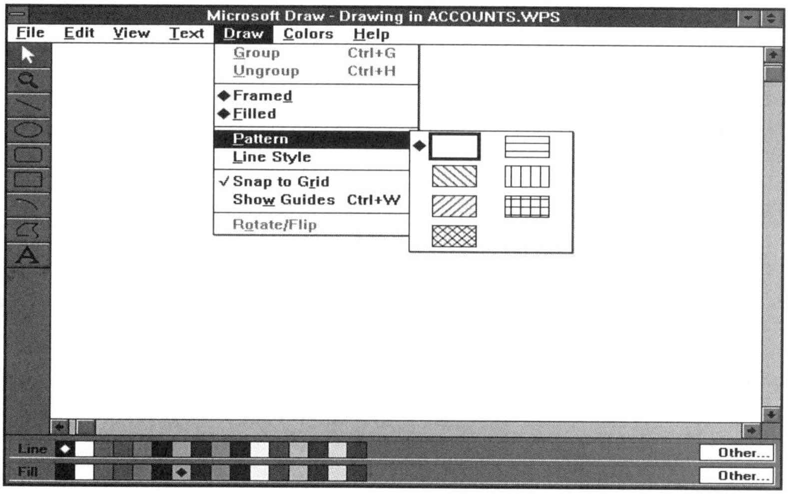

Figure 6.7   Microsoft Draw offers many pattern and line styles.

Microsoft Draw also offers many line styles and thicknesses. As with most options, you can change the line style before or after creating an object. To select a line style, select Line Style from the Draw pull-down menu, and then select the line style or thickness you want. To change the line style of an already existing object, select the object before choosing the new line style.

Tip: To enter a line thickness larger than 10 points, select Other from the Line Style cascading menu, and then manually type the line thickness, up to 250 points.

Rotating and Flipping Objects

Often, you'll want to change the orientation of an object you've drawn. For example, suppose you're creating a compass and need to have arrows pointing north, south, east, and west. There's no need to draw four different arrows. You can draw one arrow, as in Figure 6.8, copy it, and then use Microsoft Draw's Rotate/Flip function to change the arrow's orientation for each compass point (see Figure 6.9).

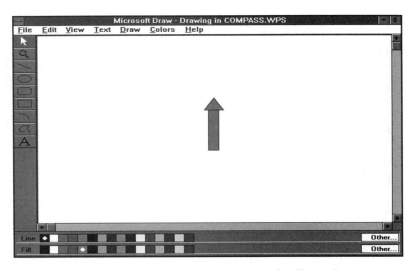

Figure 6.8   Objects, like this arrow, can be flipped or rotated to change their orientation.

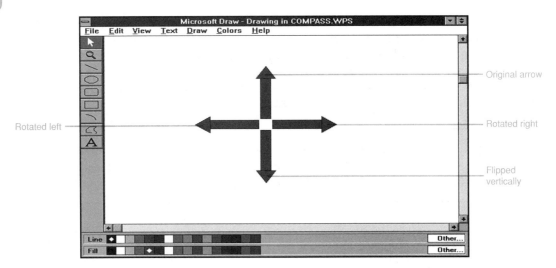

Figure 6.9   After copying the original arrow three times, each copy was rotated or flipped to create this compass.

The following Quick Steps detail how to use Rotate/Flip.

 Using Rotate/Flip

1. Use your mouse to select the object you want to rotate or flip.

   Works marks the object as selected.

2. Select Rotate/Flip from the Draw pull-down menu

   The Draw/Flip cascading menu appears.

3. In the cascading menu, select Rotate Left, Rotate Right, Flip Horizontal, or Flip Vertical.

   The selected object rotates or flips to its new orientation. □

Grouping Objects

91

When you create an image made up of many individual objects, you run into trouble when you try to move the image. For example, suppose you create a face in your drawing, and then decide that you want to move the face to a different part of the screen. Because the face is made up of several individual objects, you might think you'd have to move each object one at a time, reconstructing the face in its new location. But Microsoft Draw provides a clever alternative. It allows you to combine many objects into a single object, which can then be moved around the screen as one piece. To group a series of objects, first go from object to object, selecting each object by clicking on it while holding down the Shift key. The object's handles appear, letting you know it's selected (see Figure 6.10). When you've selected the objects, select Group from the Draw pull-down menu. Works combines the selected objects into a single object (see Figure 6.11). You can ungroup a grouped object by first selecting the group and then select Ungroup from the Draw menu.

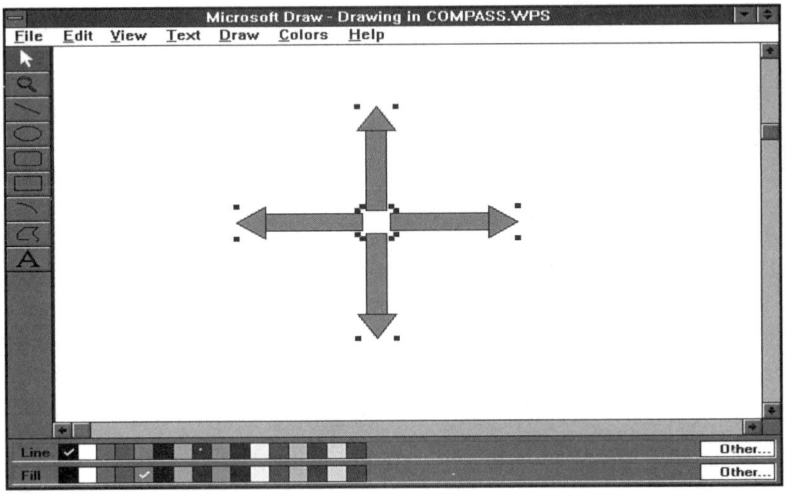

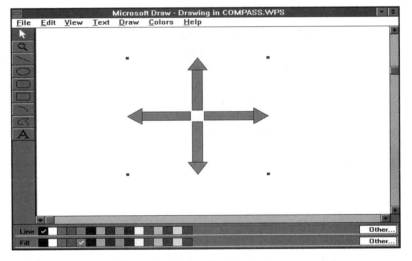

Figure 6.10   To group objects, first select each object by
holding down Shift while clicking on it.

Figure 6.11   After selecting all objects to group, choosing
Group from the Draw pull-down menu does the trick.

The following Quick Steps detail grouping objects.

 Grouping Objects

1. Click on the first object to select it.	Works displays the object's handles, indicating it's selected.
2. Holding down the Shift key, click on the next object in the group.	Works marks the object, as selected, by displaying its handles.
3. Repeat step 2 for each object in the group.	Works marks each object as selected.
4. Select Group from the Draw pull-down menu.	Works combines the selected objects into a single object. □

93

Importing Other Picture Types

You probably have a collection of pictures that were created with programs other than Microsoft Draw. Frequently, you may want to add one or more of these images to your Works documents. To do this, first *import* (convert and load) the picture into Microsoft Draw (see Figure 6.12). You'll need to provide specific information about the graphic in the Import Picture dialog box, which is accessed through the File menu. Some picture types that can be imported into Microsoft Draw include those with .BMP, .PCX, .TIF, and .WMF file name extensions.

Use the following Quick Steps to import pictures into Microsoft Draw.

 Importing a Picture

1. Select Import Picture from the File pull-down menu.	The Import Picture dialog box appears.

2. If you need to switch to a different directory, find the directory in the Directories list box, select it, and click on the OK button.

Works switches to the new directory.

3. Choose a graphics file from the Files list box.

Works highlights the selected file.

4. Click on the OK button or press Enter.

Works imports the graphics file.

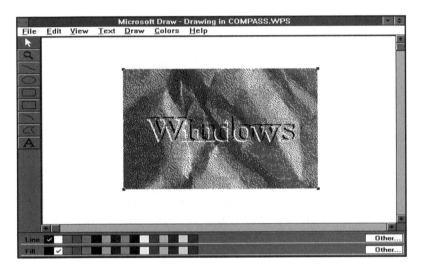

Figure 6.12   You can import other picture types into Microsoft Draw.

 Note: When you import a picture from another graphics program, Works loads it as a single object.

Exit and Return

When you're through creating your drawing, you'll want to leave Microsoft Draw and paste the picture into your document. To do this, select Exit and Return from the File pull-down menu. Works asks if you want to update your word processor file. Select the Yes button to paste the drawing into your document. Select the No button to return to your word processor without pasting the drawing into your document.

If you'd like to update your word processor document with the new drawing without leaving Microsoft Draw, select Update from the File pull-down menu (see Figure 6.13). Works pastes a copy of the current drawing into your document and then returns you to Microsoft Draw.

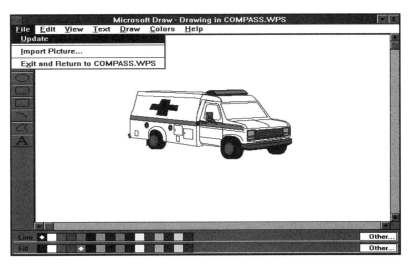

Figure 6.13   Use Exit and Return to paste a copy of the drawing into your document and leave Microsoft Draw.

What You Have Learned

- ▶ Microsoft Draw can be started only from within the word processor by selecting <u>D</u>rawing from the Insert pull-down menu.

- ▶ Microsoft Draw provides nine tool buttons that, when clicked on, select various drawing functions.

- ▶ Most objects are composed of frames and fills, the colors of which can be changed by selecting the Line and Fill color palettes.

- ▶ Objects can be easily aligned with each other by using the Snap to G<u>r</u>id function, available in the Draw pull-down menu.

- ▶ Like words in a word processor document, objects in Microsoft Draw can be cut, deleted, copied, and pasted.

- ▶ You can select various patterns and line styles from <u>P</u>attern and <u>L</u>ine Style in the Draw pull-down menu.

- ▶ The Rotate and Flip functions let you change an object's orientation.

- ▶ Objects can be grouped into a single object to make them easier to move.

- ▶ Several picture types can be imported into Microsoft Draw by using the <u>I</u>mport Picture function, available in the File pull-down menu.

- ▶ When you exit Microsoft Draw, you can have your drawing pasted into your word processor document. You can also paste the drawing into your document by choosing <u>U</u>pdate from the File pull-down menu.

Database Basics

In This Chapter

- ▶ *Understanding databases*
- ▶ *Getting started*
- ▶ *Viewing a database*
- ▶ *Adding, deleting, and moving fields*
- ▶ *Entering and editing data*
- ▶ *Printing a database*

Whenever you have many similar items to keep track of, you've got a good application for a database. A database can keep track of almost anything, from your favorite recipes or a Christmas card list, to a customer information file or a parts inventory. In this chapter, you'll learn what makes up a database file and how to get started with the Microsoft Works database program. By the end of this chapter, you'll be ready to create a database of your own.

Fields, Records, and Databases

A database is a collection of *records*, each of which comprises a number of *fields*. If you've little experience with computer databases, that last sentence probably left you reeling. But believe it or not, while you may not have used a computer database before, you've been using databases of one sort or another all your life. Let's look at a real-life example. Suppose you have an address book with 100 pages and suppose that each page has a line for a person's name, street address, city, state, ZIP code, and telephone number. You could call the entire book a database, each page of the book a record, and each line on a page—name, street address, city, and so on—a field. Your address book has room for 200 addresses; in other words, it'll hold a maximum of 200 records.

A computer database is similar. The main difference is that the information in a computer database is stored on a disk not in a book, and the information is displayed on a screen not on a page. Because the information that makes up a computer database is so readily available to your computer, you have much more control over the information than you would have if it was stored in a book. For example, the computer can almost instantly find any record you want or total values in certain fields. If you're still a little fuzzy about what makes up a database, Figure 7.1 ought to make it a little clearer.

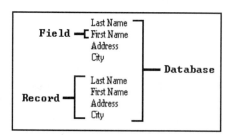

Figure 7.1   A database is a collection of records, each of which comprises a number of fields.

FYIdea: You can easily transfer data between different database programs by importing and exporting the data as comma-delimited text files. Works' Save As dialog box has a selection for this file type under the Save File as Type list box. The Open dialog box has a similar option.

The Database Screen

When you first start the database program, you see the screen shown in Figure 7.2 (unless you've changed to list view; see "Viewing a Database," later in this chapter, for more information on that option). The database screen consists of the following elements:

▷ The Menu bar at the top provides access to all the database functions.

▷ Below the Menu bar is the Toolbar, which provides quick access to frequently used functions.

▷ Below the Toolbar is the Formula bar, which displays the text cursor's X and Y coordinates (its current position on the screen), and information about the current field.

▷ Below the Formula bar is the database workspace. It is here that your database windows appear.

99

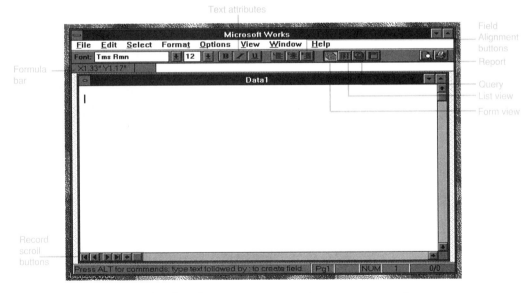

Figure 7.2   The database screen contains many controls for access to frequently used functions.

At the bottom of each database window, to the left of the horizontal scroll bar, are the Scroll buttons, which let you move easily from record to record. The Scroll button functions are listed in Table 7.1.

Table 7.1   Scroll Button Functions.

Icon	Function
◄	Move to first record
◄	Move to previous record
►	Move to next record
►	Move to last record

Viewing a Database

You can view the records of a Works database in one of two ways: *Form view* and *List view*. Form view, shown in Figure 7.3, displays a single record on the screen, with the fields arranged in the positions you selected. Most often, you'll use Form view to setup a database and to enter and edit data. To move from record to record in Form view, you use the scroll buttons.

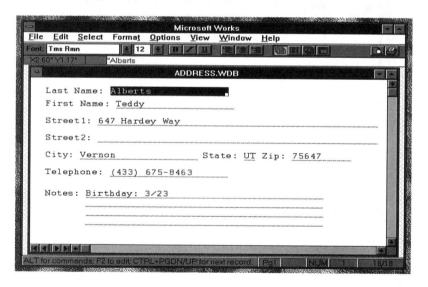

Figure 7.3   *In Form view, you can see only one record at a time.*

100

List view, shown in Figure 7.4, lets you see many records simultaneously. You'll use this view most often to see the results of a query or when you want to scan a database quickly without having to move constantly from record to record, as you do when in Form view.

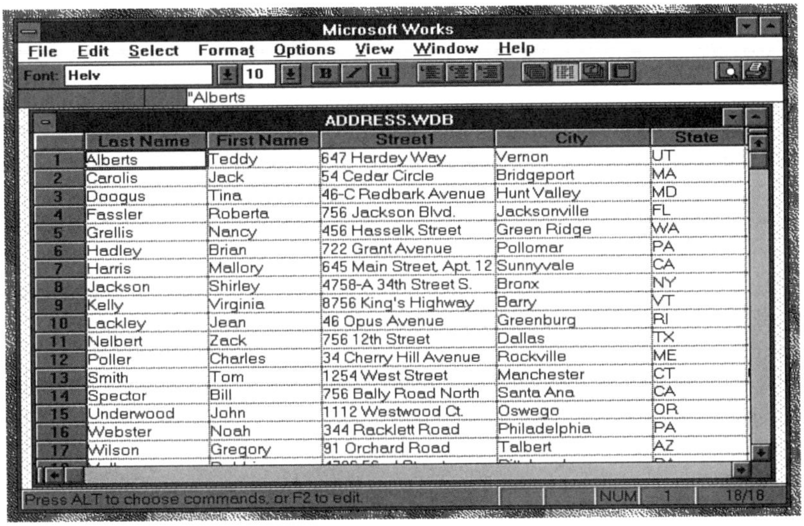

Figure 7.4   In List view, you can see many records simultaneously.

To select Form view or List view, select the appropriate button on the Toolbar. You can also select Form view or List view by selecting Form or List from the View pull-down menu.

Although you can perform many of the same functions in either view, in this chapter we will concentrate on Form view. For more information on functions particular to List view, please consult your Works for Windows manual.

Creating a New Field

The first step in starting a database is creating the form you'll use to input each record. As we said previously, a record comprises a number of fields, so creating a form for your records means defining the necessary fields. In our address book, we want to create fields for a first name, last name, street address, city, state, ZIP code, and telephone number. When creating fields, keep in mind that your database uses fields for its searches and sorts. In other words, if you expect to sort your database on a person's last name, you need a separate last name field. Likewise, if you think you'll need to search for a certain ZIP code, you need a separate ZIP code field. When creating a new database, it's a good idea to keep the fields as specific as possible so that many search and sort options are possible.

To create a new field, position the blinking text cursor where you want the field, type the field's name followed by a colon (:), and then press Enter. The Field size dialog box appears (see Figure 7.5). Enter a size for the field, both a width and height. The width is the maximum number of characters across that can be entered into a field. For example, for a street address, you'd probably want a width of at least 30. The height is the maximum number of text lines. Usually, you will stick with a height of 1. However, you might want to use a different height for something like a note field. When you enter information into a multi-line field, words automatically "wrap around" when you reach the end of a line, just as they do in a word processor.

After entering the field's width and height, press Enter. Works creates the new field and displays it on the screen, with a dotted line showing where the field's data will be typed. The dotted line is the same length as the maximum length you chose in the Field Size dialog box. (If you chose a height greater than 1, a number of dotted lines equal to the height you chose is displayed on the screen.)

Use the above procedure to create all the fields you need for your database. When you've finished, make sure you save your work by selecting <u>S</u>ave from the File menu, or by pressing Ctrl+S.

Remember that creating new fields is a lot like labeling the lines of that address book we spoke about. You're not actually entering names and addresses into the book, but rather are defining where the names and addresses will go once all the fields are created. Later, you'll actually create records by entering data into each field, just as you would fill your address book by writing in the names and addresses of the people you want to include.

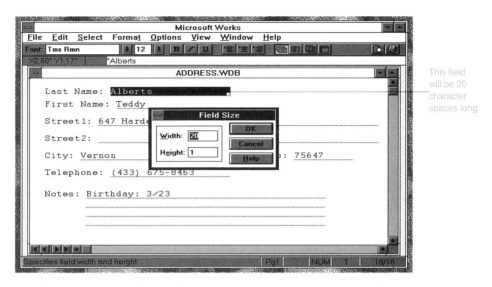

This field will be 20 character spaces long

Figure 7.5   The Field Size dialog box lets you set a field's size.

103

The following Quick Steps review the procedure for creating new fields.

Creating New Fields

1. Click the mouse pointer on the database window.

   The insertion cursor appears where you clicked.

2. Type a name for the field, followed by a colon (for example, "Last Name:").

   The name appears both on the screen and in the Formula bar.

3. Press Enter or click on the check mark in the Formula bar.

   The Field Size dialog box appears.

4. If you want to use the default sizes (20 characters long and one line high), press Enter or click on the OK button.

   The finished field appears on the screen.

5. If you don't want the default size, change the sizes shown in the dialog box, and then press Enter or click on the OK button.

   A field of your chosen size appears on the screen.

Tip: Every field name in your database must be unique. If you need to enter similar field names, use numbers to distinguish between them. For example, use field names like "Street1" and "Street2" for multiple-line addresses.

 Note: The length or height of a field cannot exceed 325.

Moving a Field

When you're first creating new fields for your database records, don't worry too much about their position. Every field can be easily moved to a different position at any time, even after you've entered data into the field. In fact, it's so easy to move fields that you can experiment with different screen layouts, moving fields around until you get exactly the screen layout you like. This is a lot like moving furniture around a room; except that fields don't weigh as much! Simply click on the field with your mouse and drag it to the desired position. The following Quick Steps detail this procedure.

Moving a Field

1. Select the field by clicking on it with your mouse pointer.	Works highlights the field.
2. Place the mouse pointer over the selected field.	The pointer changes into a hand.
3. Hold down the left mouse button while moving the hand.	An outline of the field follows the hand (see Figure 7.6).
4. Release the left mouse button.	The selected field appears under the hand cursor.

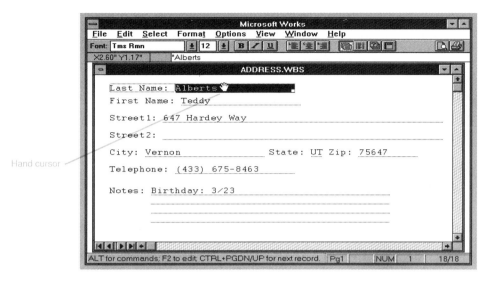

Hand cursor

Figure 7.6   When you grab a field with the hand cursor, its outline follows the hand around the screen.

Types of Data

The Works database program allows you to use three types of data in your database files:

- ▶ Text
- ▶ Numbers
- ▶ Formulas

Text comprises a string of characters (either letters or numbers), such as a person's name or address. You cannot perform calculations on or with text entries.

Numbers are values that can be used in calculations. An example would be an inventory count or the price of a piece of merchandise.

Formulas use the values in other fields to calculate a final value. When you enter a formula into a field, the formula's result is shown in the field, whereas the formula itself appears in the Formula bar.

For the most part, you'll use only simple formulas, such as sums or products, in your databases. However, Works supplies mathematical functions for calculating more esoteric values, such as logarithms, future values, and depreciation of an item over a specific period. A complete list of formulas you can use in your databases is found in Appendix A of your Works manual.

Entering Data into a Field

When you've got all your fields created, you'll want to start entering data. Figure 7.7 shows how our address book database might look before you enter any data. At this point, the database is nothing more than a group of empty records. To make it useful, we now need to enter all the addresses and phone numbers of the people we want in the database.

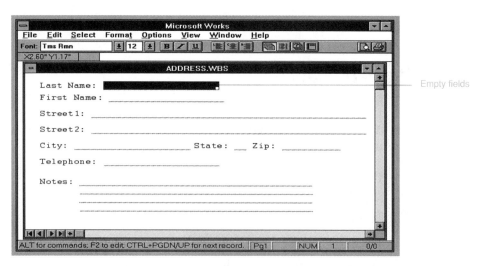

Empty fields

Figure 7.7   An address database is handy for keeping track of friends or business contacts.

Entering Text

To enter text into a field, select the field (not the field name) to select it. Then just type in your entry. For example, to enter the last name

"Smith" into the database, select the line following the field name "Last Name:", and then type `Smith`. Figure 7.8 shows the result. Notice that what you type also appears in the Formula bar above the window. When you press Enter, or click on the check mark in the Formula bar, to complete the entry, Works adds a double-quote to the beginning of the word "Smith," indicating that this field contains a string rather than a numerical value or a formula.

> **Note:** You can also move a field by using your keyboard. First, select the field by pressing direction keys until the field name is highlighted. Then select Position Field from the Edit pull-down menu. Use the direction keys to move the field, pressing Enter when the field is positioned where you want it.

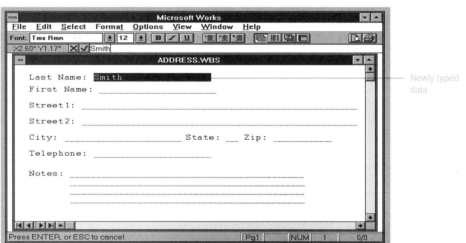

Figure 7.8   After selecting a field, you can type your data.

Entering Numbers

"Smith" is obviously a text string rather than a number. After all, it's made up only of letters. But what about something like a ZIP code? How does Works know whether the numbers you enter as a ZIP code is a text string or a value upon which it can perform calculations? You'll probably want to identify ZIP codes as text fields in order to search or sort on them, rather than calculate.

To enter a number, select the field and type the number. To tell Works to treat the number as a text string, simply enter a double-quote before you type the number. Entering a quote before a text number is especially important if the number starts with one or more zeroes, because if Works thinks the entry is a value rather than a text string, it will remove all leading zeroes. A ZIP code like "06040" would become "6040" when you pressed Enter. That's sure to confuse the Post Office. (Another way to be sure that Works doesn't delete leading zeroes is to format the field as a leading-zero field. We'll cover this and other formatting functions in the next chapter.) If you enter the number without the quote, Works will treat the number as a value upon which it can perform calculations.

Entering Formulas

Entering formulas into fields is a little more complicated. To tell Works that the entry is a formula, rather than text, precede the entry with an equals sign (=). An example of a formula is "=Balance forward+Total charges–Total credits," which calculates a new account balance, as shown in Figure 7.9. When you enter a formula, Works shows the result of the formula in the field. You can see the formula itself in the Formula bar.

The following table lists the allowed operators for formulas.

Table 7.2   Mathematical Operators.

Operator	Function
+	Addition
–	Subtraction
*	Multiplication
/	Division
^	Exponentiation

Moving From Field to Field

When entering data, press the Tab key on your keyboard to move easily from one field to the next. When you press Tab from the last field, all the data on your screen disappears, and you're again presented with a blank record. What happened to the data you entered? Don't panic; it's still there, in the previous record. You're now looking at the next empty record, #2. The number of your record, and the number of the total existing records in the database, is always indicated in the lower right corner of the workspace (see Figure 7.9).

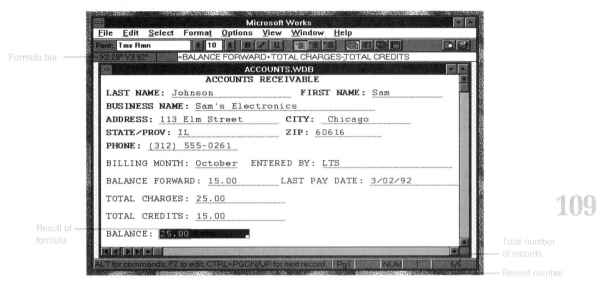

Formula bar

Result of formula

Total number of records

Record number

Figure 7.9   A field containing a formula shows the result of the formula. Works displays the formula itself in the Formula bar.

109

Editing Field Entries

Once you've entered several records, you can use the Scroll buttons, described earlier, and Ctrl+PgUp/PgDn to move through the records of your database. When you review your records, you may find data that needs to be updated or corrected. It's easy to change the data in a field by either replacing the entire entry or editing the existing entry.

To replace the entry, select it and then type a new entry. The new data replaces the old. If you want to edit the existing entry, after you select it, press F2 on your keyboard. You can then edit the entry in the Formula bar, using all the regular editing keys, such as the direction arrows, the Backspace and Delete keys. When you've finished editing the entry, press Enter (or click on the check mark on the Formula bar) to complete the changes.

Adding and Deleting Fields

You can add or delete fields in your database any time, even after you've already entered data. When you add a new field, the field is added automatically to every record in the database. For example, suppose we have 30 people entered into our address book database. Now, we add a birthday field to the first record in the database. Although we added the field to the first record, Works automatically copies the new field into all 30 records. This is because, except for the data entered into the fields, every database record must be identical.

To add a field to a database, select the database window, type the field's name, press Enter, and set the field's size. The new field appears in every record. Once you create the new field, you can move it wherever you like on the screen.

To delete a field from a record, highlight the field's name, and then press Delete, followed by Enter. Works asks if you want to delete the data in the field. If you answer Yes, the field and all the data associated with the field, are deleted from your database.

Adding a field to a database isn't particularly dangerous. You just end up with a lot of empty fields that need data. Deleting a field from a database, however, requires careful consideration. When you delete a field from one record, you're actually deleting it from every record. Moreover, when you delete the field, you also delete all the information that was stored in the field, in every record. Because you can inadvertently erase a lot of data with this function, Works always warns you before it deletes a field (see Figure 7.10).

Figure 7.10   Works warns you before it deletes a field.

110

To add and delete a field, use the following Quick Steps.

 Adding a Field

1. Position the blinking text cursor where you want the new field.	Works sets the position for the new field.
2. Type the field's name, followed by a colon, and press Enter.	The Field Size dialog box appears.
3. Enter the new field's width and height into the Width and Height text boxes, and press Enter.	Works adds the new field to the database in the selected position. □

 Deleting a Field

1. Select the field you want to delete.	Works highlights the field, indicating the field is selected.
2. Select Delete Field from the Edit pull-down menu.	Works asks whether it's okay to delete the data in the selected field.
3. If you don't mind losing the data in the selected field, click on the OK button or press Enter.	Works deletes the field, and its associated data, from every record in the database. □

111

 Warning: When you delete a field, you lose the field's data in every record.

Printing a Database

Just as with a word processor document, you can print the contents of a database. But because database files are set up differently from other text documents, some special rules apply. For example, you can print a database in Form view or List view. When you print a database in Form view, only one record is printed on each page, In other words, if you have 100 records in your database, you will get 100 pages when you print it (unless each record takes up more than one page).

In List view printing, the records of your database are printed one to a line, with one field following another. If the records are wider than the width of the paper, Works continues the records to another page. For example, suppose that a line on your page can hold a maximum of 60 characters. If your database records are 100 characters wide, Works prints the first 60 characters on the first page and the remaining 40 characters on the next, so that, when you lay the pages side-by-side, you can see the entire record. If your database contains more records than will fit on a page, Works first prints all the left-hand pages, then the right-hand pages. Because of how Works handles database printing, you can print a database of any width or height.

112

 Printing a Database in List View

1. Click on the List View button or press F9.

   Works switches the database to List view.

2. Select <u>P</u>rint from the File menu or press Ctrl+P.

   The Print dialog box appears.

3. Click on the OK button or press Enter.

   Works prints the database. □

Using the database report feature, you can choose exactly which fields will appear in a printed report. This allows you to design reports that meet many needs. Database reporting is covered in Chapter 9.

 To learn more about printing a database document, see Chapter 5.

What You Have Learned

▶ A database is a collection of records, each of which comprises a number of fields.

▶ The database Scroll buttons, located to the left of the horizontal scroll bar, let you move easily from record to record.

▶ You can view a Works database in Form view, which shows records one to a screen, or in List view, which allows you to see many records simultaneously.

▶ To create a new field, select the database window, type the field's name followed by a colon, and press Enter.

▶ To move a field, place the mouse cursor over the field, and then, while holding down the left mouse button, drag the field to its new location, or select Position Field from the Edit menu and use the direction keys.

▶ A Works database can contain three types of data: text, numbers, and formulas.

▶ To enter data into a field, select the field, type the entry, and press Tab or Enter.

▶ You must place a double-quote in front of numbers that you want Works to treat as text.

▶ You can edit the data in a field by selecting the field, pressing F2, and then making your changes.

▶ Works lets you add or delete fields at any time.

▶ Works prints your database differently, depending on whether you're in Form view or List view.

113

Advanced Database Functions

In This Chapter

▶ *Selecting records and fields*
▶ *Changing field names and sizes*
▶ *Setting field alignment and format*
▶ *Automatically entering dates and times*
▶ *Adding labels and notes*
▶ *Sorting a database*
▶ *Deleting records*
▶ *Searching for records*
▶ *Hiding records and fields*
▶ *Querying a database*

Now that you know how to set up a database file and how to enter and edit data, it's time to look at the more sophisticated things you can do with the Works database program. In this chapter, you'll learn how to manipulate database records in a variety of ways, including sorting records, deleting records, searching for records, and more. In addition, you'll learn the basic procedures for querying your databases. You'll also learn to modify a database's configuration by changing field names, sizes, and alignments.

Selecting Records

When you want to perform some function on a record, such as copying or deleting, you must first highlight the record. How you do this depends upon whether you're in Form view or List view. In Form view, the record currently on-screen automatically is selected (highlighted) by Works. In other words, to select a record in Form view, you need only bring it up on the screen.

If you need to work on more than one record simultaneously, you must switch to List view by clicking on the List view button on the Toolbar, or by selecting List from the View pull-down menu or pressing F9. In List view, you can highlight data in your database in one of several ways:

▶ To highlight a single record, click on the record number shown to the left of the window. Or, place the cursor on the desired record and choose Record from the Select menu.

▶ To highlight a single field in every record, click on the field's name shown at the top of the window. Or, place the cursor on the desired field and choose Field from the Select menu.

▶ To highlight any portion of one or more records, place the mouse cursor over the upper left cell of the desired range, hold down the left mouse button, and drag the mouse cursor over the entries you want to highlight. From the keyboard, first press F8 and then use the direction keys to highlight the desired cells.

▶ To highlight an entire database, click on the blank button to the left of the field names. Or, choose All from the Select menu.

Figure 8.1 shows a block of records highlighted in List view.

Changing a Field Name

After you've constructed a database and used it for a while, you may think of more appropriate names for one or more of the database's fields. Luckily, you can change a field name without affecting data that you have already entered. To change a field name in Form view, select the field name, type a new name followed by a colon, and press Enter. Works replaces the old field name with the new one.

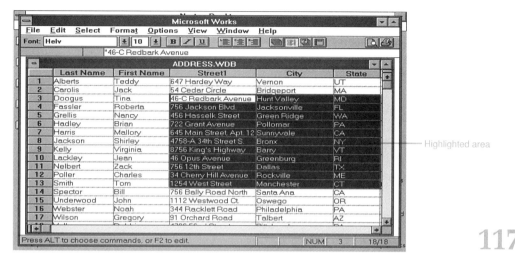

Figure 8.1   In List view, you can highlight any portion of one or more records.

Although it's easiest to change a field name while in Form view, you can change field names in List view too. Use the following Quick Steps to change a field name in List view.

 Changing a Field Name in List View

1. At the top of the document window, select the field name you want to change.	Works highlights the field's column.
2. Select Field Name from the Edit menu.	The Field Name dialog box appears, as shown in Figure 8.2.
3. Type the new field name.	The new name appears in the Name text box.
4. Press Enter or click on the OK button.	Works replaces the old field name with the new one. □

Type in a new field name followed by a colon

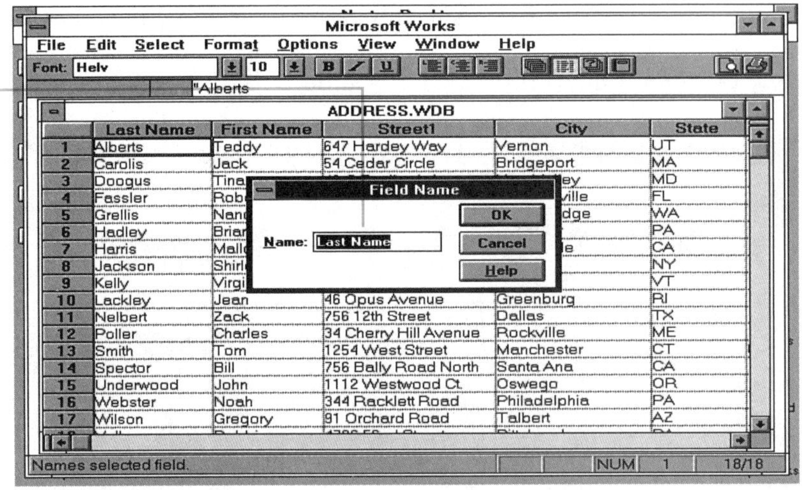

Figure 8.2   *The Field Name dialog box lets you change a field name while in List view.*

118

Changing a Field Size

When you start using a new database, you may discover that you've allotted too little or too much space for one or more fields. If you have too little space set aside for a field, you may have to use abbreviations to fit data into the field. Too much, and you waste precious viewing space on the screen.

To change a field's size while in Form view, select the field's data line. Works highlights the field and places a small white box in the lower right corner. Place your mouse cursor over the box, hold down the left mouse button, and drag the field to its new size.

Although the drag method is quick, you can't easily judge the exact size of the changed field. Use the following Quick Steps to change a field in Form view to an exact measurement.

 Changing a Field's Size in Form View

1. Select the field you want to change. (Select the data line, not the field name.)

Works highlights the field.

2. Select Field Size from the Format pull-down menu.

The Field Size dialog box appears, as shown in Figure 8.3.

3. Type the new field width.

The new width appears in the Width text box.

4. Press the Tab key and then type the new field height.

The new height appears in the Height text box.

5. Press Enter or click on the OK button.

Works changes the field to its new size.

Figure 8.3   The Field Size dialog box allows you to change a field to the exact size you require.

119

You can change the displayed width of a field in List view by placing your mouse pointer over the right edge of the field name (the pointer changes to double arrows), holding down the left mouse button, and dragging the edge of the field to the desired size.

Note: Changing the size of a field in List view affects only how the field is shown in the list. When you return to Form view, you still have the same amount of space for entering data into the field.

Setting Field Alignment

Like the paragraphs that make up a word processing document, the fields that make up a record in your database can be aligned in different ways—specifically, left justified, centered, or right justified. When you type data into a field, Works makes certain assumptions about how the data should be aligned. For example, text data is automatically left justified, and numbers are right justified, so they line up properly in a list.

To change the alignment of a field, in either Form or List view, select the field and then click on one of the field alignment buttons on the Toolbar. Works realigns the data according to the new setting. You can also change field alignment by selecting Style from the Format menu. Figure 8.4 shows alignment changes in List view.

> **Note:** When you change a field's alignment, you change the alignment in every record. The new alignment appears in both Form and List view.

Field alignment buttons

Figure 8.4   Use the field alignment buttons on the Toolbar to change a field's alignment.

Setting Field Formats

The fields that make up the records of your database can be formatted in many ways (Figure 8.5), allowing you to display the data in its most appropriate form. For example, when entering numbers with decimal points, you usually want the numbers to line up on the decimal point, whereas text usually looks best left justified. Works offers the following formats:

General: What you type into a field stays exactly as you entered it.

Fixed: Numbers are formatted to a fixed number of decimal places, for example, 234.76. The default is two decimal places, but it can be changed.

Currency: Numbers are preceded by a dollar sign and are displayed with two decimal places, for example, $54.98.

Comma: Long numbers include commas, for example, 1,345,654.

Percent: Numbers are displayed as a percentage, for example, 45.23%.

Exponential: Numbers are shown in scientific notation, for example, 1.37E+03.

Leading zeroes: Leading zeroes on all entries are maintained, for example, 00674.

True/False: A value of 0 yields FALSE. Any other value yields TRUE.

Time/Date: Dates and times are formatted according to the settings in the Time/Date dialog box, for example, 1/21/91 or January 21, 1991.

121

Figure 8.5   Works can display fields in many formats.

To set a field's format, first select the field. Then choose the desired format from the Format pull-down menu. If a format dialog box appears (some formats use a dialog box, others don't), select the desired settings, then press Enter or click on the OK button. Works displays the field in its new format.

You can have a field displayed in bold, italic, or under-lined text, as well as in different fonts and character sizes, by selecting those attributes from the Toolbar or selecting <u>S</u>tyle from the Format menu. Refer to Chapter 4 for more information.

Entering the Current Date or Time

If you're going to use Works in your business, you'll probably enter many times and dates into your database records. Works provides a quick way to get the current date or time into a field. To enter the current date quickly, hold down the Ctrl key and type a semicolon. To enter the current time quickly, hold down the Ctrl and Shift keys, and then type a semicolon.

Works can display times and dates in a number of formats, as we discussed in an earlier section. After you've entered a date or time, you can reformat it any way you like by selecting <u>T</u>ime/Date from the Format pull-down menu. Now choose the desired format from the Time/Date dialog box, shown in Figure 8.6.

Figure 8.6   The Time/Date dialog box lets you choose from many time and date formats.

Entering Labels and Notes

Often, you'll want to add explanatory text to your database's form. This text might be a simple label or instructional text, designed to help a user enter data. When in Form view, you can place labels or notes anywhere on the screen. Simply position the text cursor on the screen where you want the text placed. Then type the text and press Enter. Make sure you don't end the text with a colon. A colon signals Works to create a new field.

As with a field, you can reposition a label or note by placing the mouse cursor over the text, holding down the left mouse button, and dragging the text to a new location. You can also move a label or note by selecting Position Field from the Edit menu and then the direction keys to reposition the item.

> **Warning:** If you add a colon to a label or note, Works will think you are trying to define a new field, and the Field Size dialog box will appear when you press Enter. To correct your error, select the Cancel button, then remove the colon from the text.

123

Sorting Records

In most databases, it's helpful to sort records into some type of logical order. In an address database, for example, you'd probably want to sort the database on people's last names. You especially need to sort a database before printing it, since you obviously can't use the computer's search functions to find records on a print out.

Works allows you to sort your database, using up to three fields as *keys*. In an address database, you'd want to sort, at least, by using the last name field. You might also want to sort using the first name field as well, in case you have several people with the same last name.

For example, let's say that, in our example address database, we've got 1000 records, including records for Alan Birch, who lives in Springfield; Thomas Birch, who lives in Denver; Gail Smith, who lives in Kansas City; and another Gail Smith, who lives in Dallas. If we were to sort the database using only the last names, the records for Alan Birch and Thomas Birch may not end up in exactly the right order. Because both last names are the same, and because we aren't considering their first names in the sort, Thomas may end up before Alan.

A similar situation exists for the two Gails, but in their case, sorting on both their first and last names is still not enough, since then we may end up with Kansas City before Dallas. For a large database, one that may have many duplicate names, it would be helpful to have records listed in order of their town as well as their names.

So, to make sure our database is in exactly the right order, we sort on three keys in this order: Last name, first name, and city. After the sort, our four example records would be in this order:

Birch, Alan	Springfield
Birch, Thomas	Denver
Smith, Gail	Dallas
Smith, Gail	Kansas City

To sort a database, use the following Quick Steps.

Q Sorting a Database

1. Choose Sort Records from the Select pull-down menu.	The Sort Records dialog box appears, as shown in Figure 8.7.
2. Type the name of the field on which you want to sort, if necessary.	The field name appears in the 1st Field text box.
3. Choose the order in which you want to sort (Ascending or Descending). If you want to search on an additional field, press Tab, and then enter the second field name.	The second field name appears in the 2nd Field text box.
4. Repeat step 3 if you want to search on a third field.	The third field name appears in the 3rd Field text box.
5. Press Enter or click on the OK button.	Works sorts the database according to your criteria. □

The Sort Records dialog box also lets you choose between *ascending* or *descending* order. Sorting in ascending order (for example, A to Z) is the default selection. However, you can switch to descending order (Z-A) by selecting the Descend option button associated with the field on which you're sorting.

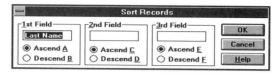

Figure 8.7   You can sort a database using up to three fields as keys.

FYIdea: When preparing a mailing list, sort your records by zip code. This "presorting" of your mail may make you eligible for discounts from the Post Office.

125

Deleting Records

As your database gets larger, you may want to trim it down by deleting records no longer needed. To delete a record while in Form view, bring the record up onto the screen and then select Delete Record from the Edit menu. Works removes the record from the database. To delete a record while in List view, select any field in the record and select Delete Record/Field from the Edit pull-down menu. When the Delete dialog box appears, make sure the Record option button is selected and then press Enter or click on the OK button.

Warning: When you delete a record, it is gone forever. Works gives no warning and allows no second chances. Moreover, when in List view, if you have the Field option button of the Delete dialog box selected (rather than the Record option button), you'll irrevocably lose all the data in the selected field when you activate the delete function. Again, Works gives *no warning*, so use this option carefully.

Searching for Records

One advantage of a database is the ease with which you can locate a particular record. Works can search your database records in a flash, finding any record almost instantly. To find a specific record, first select <u>F</u>ind from the Select pull-down menu. When the Find dialog box appears, type the text for which to search. Then select either the Next <u>R</u>ecord or <u>A</u>ll Records option button. Finally, press Enter, or click the dialog box's OK button. Works searches the database for the selected entry or entries.

Delete
function

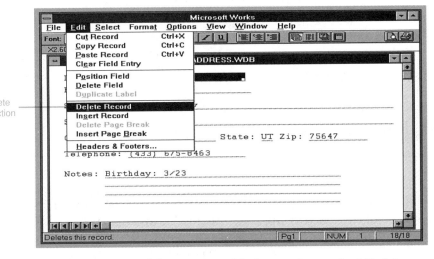

Figure 8.8   To delete a record in Form view, select Delete Record from the Edit pull-down menu.

Use the following Quick Steps to perform the Search function.

 Finding a Record

1. Choose <u>F</u>ind from the Select pull-down menu.

   The Find dialog box appears, as shown in Figure 8.9.

2. Type the text for which to search.

   The target text appears in the Find What text box.

3. Select either the Next Record or All records option button.

If you choose Next record, Works will find only the first record that matches the target text. If you choose All Records, Works will locate all matching records and hide the rest.

4. Press Enter or click on the OK button.

Works starts the search.

☐

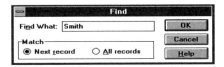

Figure 8.9   To find a record or group of records, type a target text string into the Find dialog box.

127

If you search for all matching records, Works hides every record that doesn't match the target string. To bring back the hidden records, choose Show All Records from the Select pull-down menu.

Tip: You can use *wild cards* in your target text when you want to locate records that are similar, but not identical. If you don't know how to use wild cards, consult your Works for Windows manual.

Hiding and Unhiding Records

When printing a report, making mailing labels, or putting together form letters, there may be records in your database you want to exclude. Works allows you to hide records by temporarily removing them from the current database. To hide a record in Form view, bring the record up onto the screen, and then select Hide Record from the Select pull-down menu. Works removes the record from the screen. To hide a record while in List view, place the selection cursor on any field in the record and then select Hide Record from the Select menu.

You can view hidden records by selecting S<u>w</u>itch Hidden Records from the Select menu. Works switches to the hidden records, while hiding all others from view. To restore the complete database, select Show A<u>l</u>l Records from the Select menu.

Hiding and Unhiding Fields

To give yourself more room in a database while in Form view, or to temporarily place related fields side by side in List view, you can hide field names and even entire fields. To hide a field name while in Form view, select the field name to highlight it, then select Show Field <u>N</u>ame from the Format pull-down menu, turning off the check mark displayed there. Works removes the field name from the display. To redisplay the field name, select Show Field <u>N</u>ame again, turning the option back on.

To hide quickly an entire field while in List view, place the mouse cursor over the right edge of the field name, hold down the left mouse button, and drag the edge of the field all the way to the left. When you release the button, Works removes the field from view.

Redisplaying Fields and Field Names

Redisplaying a field that's been hidden in List view is a little tricky. To do this, select <u>G</u>o To from the Select pull-down menu. When the Go To dialog box appears, choose the desired field name in the Names list box. Then press Enter or click on the OK button. Works places a cursor on the hidden field. Now, select Field Width from the Format pull-down menu, and when the Field Width dialog box appears, type a new field width, and press Enter or click on the OK button. Works redisplays the hidden field.

You don't need to remember the original width of the field, since the change you made in List view affects only the way the field is displayed in List view. The actual field width, as defined when you created your database, remains unchanged. You can verify this by switching back to Form view. If, for some reason, you want to know the field's exact width, highlight the field in Form view and then select Field Size from the Format menu. Works displays the Field Size dialog box, which contains the field's exact size.

Use the following Quick Steps to redisplay fields.

 Unhiding a Field in List View

1. Choose Go To from the Select pull-down menu.

   The Go To dialog box appears, as shown in Figure 8.10.

2. Select the desired field name in the Names list box.

   Works highlights the field.

3. Press Enter or click on the OK button.

   Works places an insertion cursor on the hidden field.

4. Select Field Width from the Format pull-down menu.

   The Field Width dialog box appears.

5. Type a new field width and press Enter, or click on the OK button.

   Works redisplays the hidden field.

129

Figure 8.10 The Go To dialog box lets you find hidden fields.

Database Querying

In most cases, the regular Find function suffices for database searches, but sometimes you may want to search for groups of records using more sophisticated criteria. With the Works Query function, you can set up complex instructions for a search. For example, you can locate all the people who live in New Jersey, have incomes greater than $30,000 per year, and have last names starting with "T." The Query function is especially helpful for putting together different types of database reports. (We'll cover reports in the next chapter.)

Setting Up a Database Query

To set up a database query, click on the Query button (the button marked with a question mark) in the Toolbar or select Query from the View menu. The screen changes to Query mode, which looks similar to Form view. In one or more fields, type the query instructions (see Figure 8.11). After you've entered the query instructions into the form, start the query by clicking on the List view button in the Toolbar or select List from the View menu. Works displays a list of all matching records.

Text string

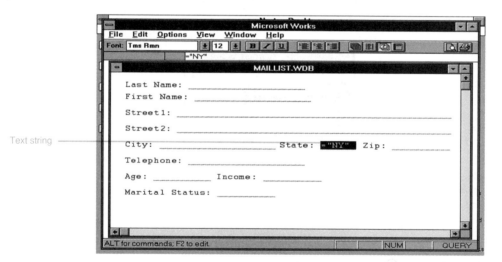

Figure 8.11   You can find all records containing a certain text string by typing the text into the appropriate field. In this example, Works will list all customers who live in NY.

To exit the query, choose Show All Records from the Select pull-down menu. Works displays all the records in the database. If you like, you can reapply the last query by choosing Apply Query from the Select menu. The following Quick Steps detail setting up a query.

Database Querying

1. Click on the Toolbar's Query button, or select Query from the View menu.	The screen changes to query mode, displaying a blank record.
2. In one or more fields, type the query instructions.	The query instructions define which records will be selected when the query is activated.
3. Start the query by clicking on the Toolbar's List view button, or by selecting List from the View menu.	Works scans the database and displays a list of all matching records. □

The following list shows some ways you can query a database, using a customer profile database as an example. Query instructions can be quite complex, so we will cover only the most common ones here.

131

▶ An instruction like ="Smith" allows you to search for any occurrence of a specific text string (see Figure 8.12). You can also write this instruction by just entering Smith without the equal sign and the quotes.

▶ An instruction like >30,000 uses the greater-than (>) operator to locate values larger than the given value (see Figure 8.13).

▶ An instruction like <"M" uses the less-than (<) operator to find all occurrences of text strings that start with letters preceding the given letter (see Figure 8.14).

▶ By combining greater-than (>) and less-than (<) operators with the AND operator (&), you can locate values or text that fall into a given range. An example is >"M"&<"T", which searches for all text strings that start with letters between M and T (see Figure 8.15).

▶ The NOT (~) operator lets you reverse an equation and look for values that don't match. For example, if ="SMITH" searches for all occurrences of Smith, then =~(="Smith") searches for all entries that aren't Smith (see Figure 8.16).

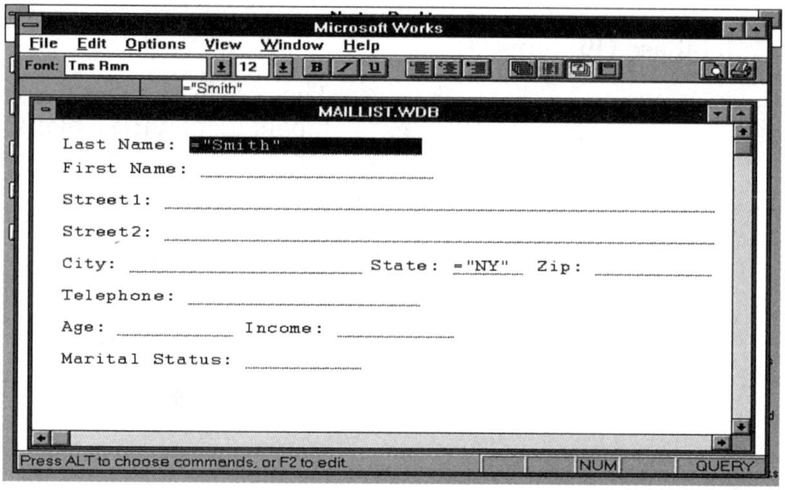

Figure 8.12   In this example, Works will list all customers named Smith who live in NY.

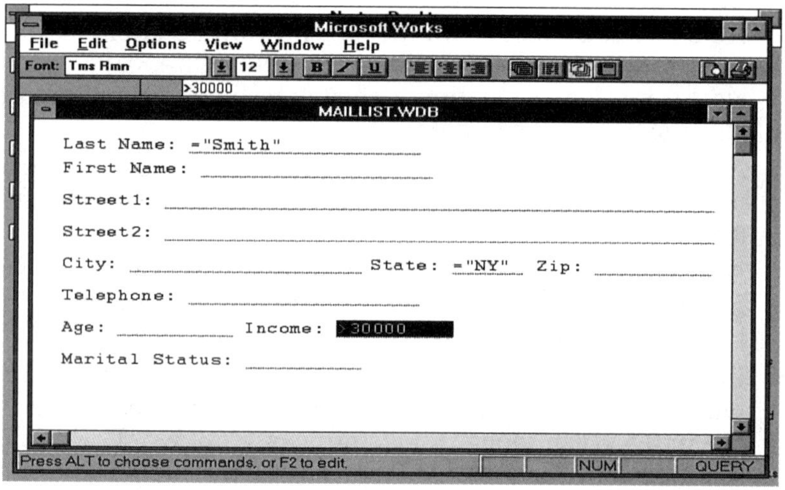

Figure 8.13   In this example, Works will list all customers named Smith who live in NY, and who have incomes greater than $30,000.

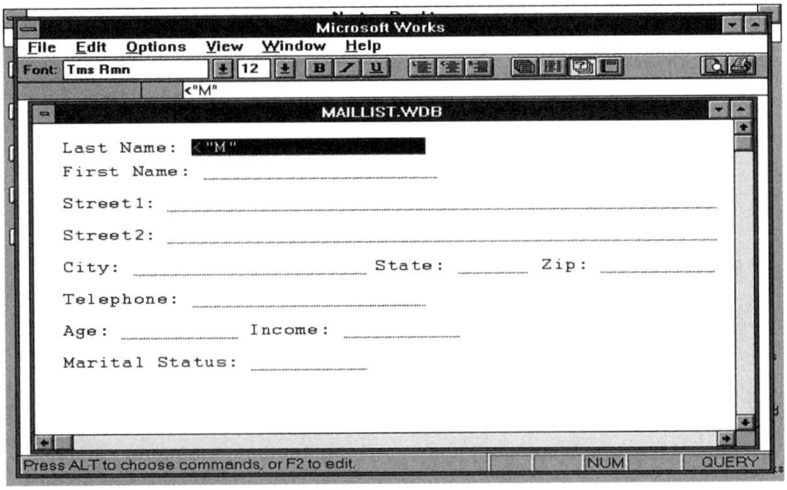

Figure 8.14   In this example, Works will list all customers whose last names start with a letter preceding "M."

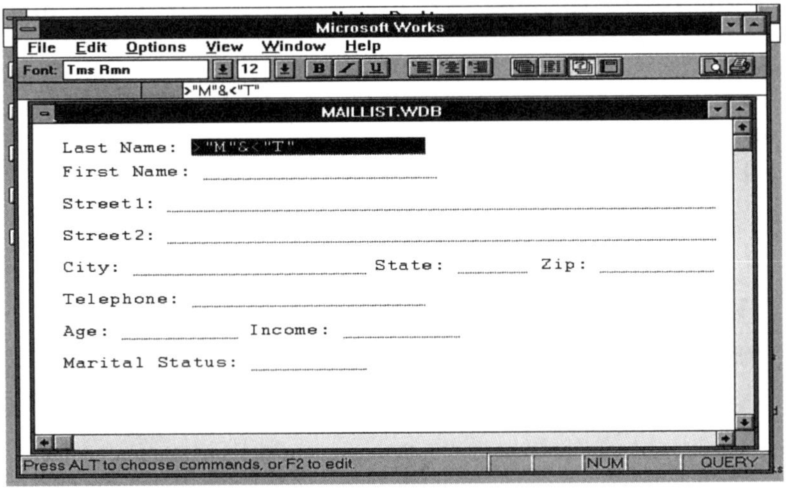

Figure 8.15   In this example, Works will list every customer whose last name starts with a letter between "M" and "T."

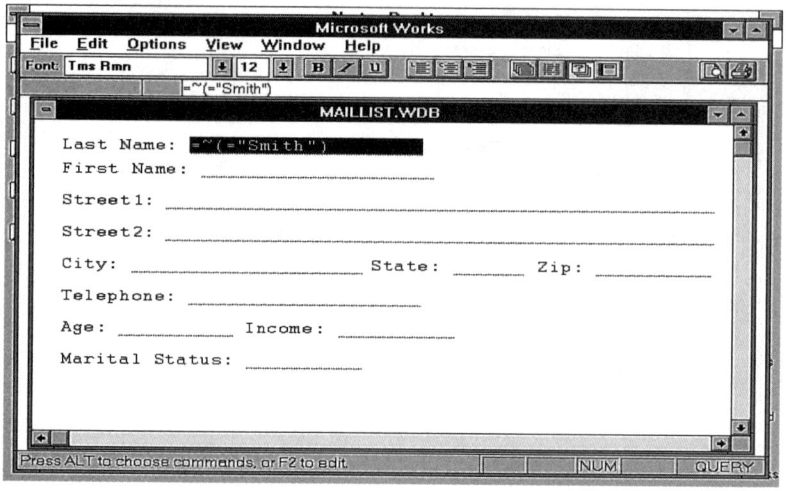

Figure 8.16   *In this example, Works will list all customers whose names are not Smith.*

134

The examples given in the figures are only a few of the most common ways you can query a database. In reality, the methods you can use are virtually endless. You can even use mathematical functions or wild cards in your query instructions. Refer to your Works for Windows manual for more information on using more complex methods.

What You Have Learned

▶ In Form view, the record on the screen is automatically highlighted. In List view, you can highlight a record by selecting the record's number.

▶ To change a field name, select it and type a new name followed by a colon.

▶ To change a field's size in Form view, select the field, and then drag the white box in the lower right corner of the field. You can change a field's size in List view by dragging the right edge of the field name to the left or right.

▶ Use the alignment buttons in the Toolbar to select left-justified, centered, or right-justified field alignment. A field can be formatted in eight ways: general, fixed, currency, comma, exponential, leading zeroes, true/false, and time/date.

▶ To add labels and notes to a database form, select the form window and type the desired text.

▶ To sort a database, choose Sort Records from the Select pull-down menu.

▶ To delete a record first select it, and then select Delete Record from the Edit pull-down menu. To find a specific record, choose Find from the Select pull-down menu and enter the target text.

▶ Works allows you to hide fields while in List view and to hide field names while in Form view. You can hide any record by first selecting the record, and then choosing Hide Record from the Select pull-down menu.

▶ When you query a database, you can search for a group of records using powerful query instructions, which allow you to use logical operators and functions.

135

Database Reporting

In This Chapter

▶ *Creating simple reports*
▶ *Understanding report definitions*
▶ *Adding and deleting rows and columns*
▶ *Adding text and instructions to a report*
▶ *Changing report column widths*
▶ *Formatting and aligning report cells*
▶ *Creating sort breaks*
▶ *Report querying*
▶ *Renaming and deleting reports*

Although you can print a database using Works' regular printing function, you sometimes will want to print specially formatted reports. The Works database report generator allows you to design many types of reports. Not only can you choose which fields to print and how they will be printed, but you can also add titles, labels, and notes. You can even do calculations and counts using the report generator's built-in arithmetic functions. Moreover, report definitions are saved with your database so once you create a report, it is available to you any time. In this chapter, you'll learn the basics of creating custom reports.

Simple Reports

The simplest report is produced by Works' regular printing function. However, by creating one of Works' standard reports, you can have more power over how your database is printed, while still keeping the report-generation process simple. To create a simple report, select Create New Report from the View menu, or click on the Toolbar's Report button. When the New Report dialog box appears, type in your report's title, select the fields you want to appear in the report, and then select the OK button. In the Report Statistics dialog box, select the fields on which you want to perform calculations. Then click on the OK button, or press Enter. Works creates the report.

138

> **Note:** If you don't have a mouse and are having a difficult time operating the dialog boxes from your keyboard, please review the section "Of Mice and Keyboards" in the Introduction.

To create a simple report, use the following Quick Steps.

 Creating a Simple Report

1. Select Create New Report from the View pull-down menu.	The New Report dialog box appears, as shown in Figure 9.1.
2. Type a title for the report.	The title appears in the Report Title text box.
3. In the Select Fields list box, choose the field you want to appear in the first column of your report, and then select the Add button.	The selected field appears in the Fields In Report list box.
4. Add other fields you want in the report, using the method described in step 3.	One by one, the selected fields appear in the Fields In Report list box.

5. When you've entered all the desired fields, click on the OK button or press Enter.

The Report Statistics dialog box appears, as shown in Figure 9.2.

6. If you'd like to perform calculations on a field, select the desired field and then click on the type of calculation desired in the Statistics group box.

Works highlights your choices.

7. If you selected fields for calculations, choose where you'd like the calculations displayed by selecting the Under each column or Together in rows option button.

Works highlights the selected button.

8. Click on the OK button or press Enter.

Works creates the new report, which you can view by clicking on the Toolbar's Print preview button.

139

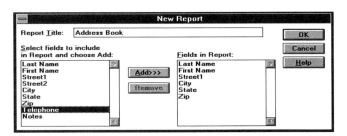

Figure 9.1   The first step in creating a report is selecting the fields to be included.

Note: Creating a report has no effect on the database data itself, except to define what data will be printed.

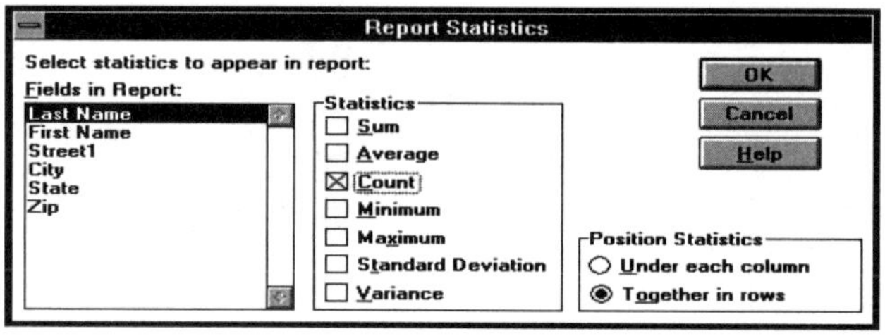

Figure 9.2   You can apply many types of calculations to the fields of a report.

The Report Definition

140

After you finish defining a new report, Works creates it and switches your database to Report view, which shows the *report definition* for the report you just defined. The report definition is made up of many fields that you must understand in order to modify your reports further.

A report definition comprises several rows, each of which is labeled along the left side of the window. Each line shows a specific type of information in your report. (A sample report definition is shown in Figure 9.3.) For example, the first Title line shows the title you typed into the New Report dialog box.

The six row types are described in the following list.

Title Rows: A typical report starts with two Title rows; one that displays the report title you entered into the New Report dialog box, and one that provides a blank line between the title and the body of the report. You can add additional heading rows if you like, which can contain whatever text you want displayed. Titles are printed once, at the top of the first page of the report.

Heading Rows: A standard report also contains two Heading rows; one that shows the field names for each column, and one that provides a blank line between the headings and the data. You can add additional heading rows, which can contain whatever text you need displayed. Heading lines are printed following the Title lines on the first page and at the top of every other page.

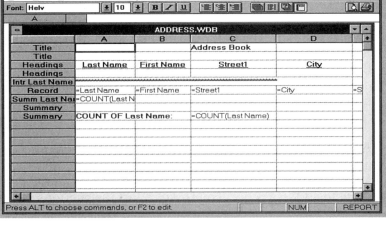

Figure 9.3   The report definition screen shows the lines that make up your report.

Record Rows: This is where the data from your database is displayed. Each cell in a Record row contains a *report instruction,* which tells Works what to display in that position. For example, if you've chosen to display a field called "Last Name," a field in the record row will contain the instruction =Last Name. A standard report has one Record row containing several different fields, but you can have as many Record rows as you like, each containing different report instructions. Record rows are always displayed following the Header rows. In the final report, they create one line for each record in your database.

Intr Rows: This type of row allows you to add blank lines or headers above data that's been arranged into *sort breaks.* For example, if you decide to sort an address database on the Last Name field and then group the names by their first letters, you could add column headings at the top of each group. In the address database example, the Intr row in your report would be labeled "Intr Last Name," because an Intr row is always identified by the field name on which the data is sorted and grouped. In Figure 9.3, the Intr row will place a row of asterisks between each group.

Summ Rows: Summ rows also help organize sorted group data by placing totals of summed fields after each group. For example, in our address database we could use the COUNT function on the Last Name field, and so display the number of names in each group. These rows act as subtotals.

Summary Rows: Summary rows display the results of calculations you performed, for the entire report. If you think of Summ rows as subtotals, then the Summary rows are the final totals. In our example of using the COUNT function to count the number of names in a group, we'd get the total number of names for the entire database in the Summary row.

Any row in a report definition can be modified by typing text or formulas into a cell. In this way, you can fine-tune your reports to display your data exactly as you need it. Later in this chapter, you'll learn how to add to a report your own report instructions and text.

Adding Rows and Columns

As you modify your report definition, you'll likely want to add extra rows or columns in order to format the report exactly to your needs. You might, for example, want to add some totals or maybe some text at the top of the report. Use the following Quick Steps to add a row.

 Adding a Row

1. Select a row name on the left side of the window.	Works highlights the chosen row.
2. Select Insert Row/Column from the Edit pull-down menu.	The Insert Row dialog box appears, as shown in Figure 9.4.
3. In the Type list box, select the type of row you want to add.	Works highlights the selected row type.
4. Click on the OK button or press Enter.	Works adds the new row in its appropriate position. □

> **Note:** Intr and Summ rows are available only in reports that contain sort breaks.

Figure 9.4   The Insert Row dialog box lets you choose from the different row types available for your report.

When adding rows to a report, Works always places the new rows in their correct positions. For example, Works places Summary rows only at the end of the report. You can, however, get Works to place a new row in a specific position with respect to other rows of the same type. For example, suppose you have two Summary rows in your report definition. You can add a Summary row between the two existing ones by highlighting the second Summary row before adding the new one. However, if you highlight a Summary row and then add a Heading row, Works places the new Heading row immediately following any existing Heading rows, *not* in the Summary row section. In this way, Works forces you to keep your reports organized logically.

143

You can also add columns to your report definitions. You might want do this in order to separate two columns with blank space or to add a new column of data. To add a new column to a report definition, first highlight the column where you want the new column placed. Then select Insert Row/Column from the Edit pull-down menu. Works places a blank column in the selected position, moving existing columns to the right.

If you want the new column to display data, you must add report instructions to the new column by typing the instructions into the appropriate cells in each row. We'll discuss report instructions later in this chapter.

Deleting Rows and Columns

Often, while revising a report definition, you'll want to remove certain rows or columns. You may, for example, want to remove a column of data from the report, or close up the columns a little by removing blank space. To delete a row or column, highlight the row or column and then select <u>D</u>elete Row/Column from the Edit pull-down menu. Works removes the chosen row or column, moving existing rows and columns up or left as required.

> **Warning:** When you select <u>D</u>elete Row/Column from the Edit menu, Works removes the highlighted row or column immediately, giving you no chance to reconsider. Before deleting a row or column, make sure you're really doing what you want to do.

Adding Text to a Report

Most reports require, besides the headings that Works automatically includes, text that describes the report in some way. For example, you might want to include your company's name and address at the top of the report or add notes explaining how data values were calculated. You can even add labels and dates. To add text to a report definition, select the cell where you want the text located, and then type the text. The text appears in the cell and is printed along with the rest of the report.

Adding Report Instructions

Report instructions tell Works what data to display in your reports. After creating a new column, for example, you'll probably want to have data from a field of your database printed in that column. To do this, you must insert a *field-entry* report instruction. You may also want to add some sort of calculation to a report, such as totalling the number of items in a field or counting the number of entries in a field. Use the following Quick Steps to add a field-entry report instruction.

 Adding a Field-Entry Instruction

1. Select the cell where you want the instruction placed.

   Works highlights the chosen cell.

2. Select Insert Field Entry from the Edit pull-down menu.

   The Insert Field Entry dialog box appears, as shown in Figure 9.5.

3. In the Fields list box, select the field whose data you want to add to the report.

   Works highlights the selected field.

4. Click on the OK button or press Enter.

   Works inserts the new instruction at the chosen location. □

145

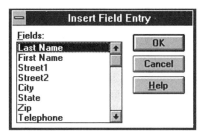

Figure 9.5 The Insert Field Entry dialog box lets you place field-entry instructions into a report definition cell.

Although you can insert a field-entry instruction anywhere in your report, it makes sense to add it only in a Record row, since it is this row that lists the field's data for every record in your database. If you enter a field-entry instruction in another type of row, only one record's data is printed, rather than the data for all records.

Adding Calculations

You can also add calculations anywhere in your report. The Works report generator supplies several built-in functions you can use. These functions are detailed in the following list.

AVG: This function averages all the numbers in a numerical field. For example, suppose you have a customer database that includes a field called "Age." The instruction =AVG(Age) would calculate the average age of your customers.

COUNT: Use this function to count the number of entries in a field. For example, suppose you had an address database with a "Telephone" field. The instruction =COUNT(Telephone) would count the number of telephone numbers entered into your database. (Any records with blank telephone fields would not be included in the count.)

MAX: This function determines the highest value in a numerical field. For example, in a customer database with a field called "Age," the instruction =MAX(Age) would display the age of the oldest customer.

MIN: This function works like MAX, except it determines the smallest value in a numerical field. For example, in a customer database with a field named "Income," the instruction =MIN(Income) would display the lowest income among all customers in the database.

STD: This function calculates standard deviation. For example, suppose you had a database of high school students with a field called "Final Score." The instruction =STD(Final Score) would calculate the standard deviation of all the students' final scores.

SUM: Use this function to add the numbers in a numerical field. For example, suppose you had a customer database with a field named "Number Ordered" that lists the number of a specific item purchased by the customer. The instruction SUM(Number Ordered) would display the total number of items ordered by all customers in the database or in a sorted group.

VAR: This function calculates the variance of values in a numeric field. For example, in a student database with a field named "Test Score," the instruction =VAR(Test Score) would calculate the variance of the scores.

Calculations must be inserted into Summ or Summary rows in order to work properly. To insert a calculation instruction into a report definition, use the following Quick Steps.

Adding a Calculation Instruction

1. Select the cell in which you want the calculation placed.

   Works highlights the cell.

2. Select Insert Field Summary from the Edit pull-down menu.

   The Insert Field Summary dialog box appears, as shown in Figure 9.6.

3. In the Fields list box, select the field on which you want to perform the calculation

   Works highlights the field.

4. In the Statistic option box, select the function you want to use.

   Works marks the function as selected.

5. Click on the OK button or press Enter.

   Works enters the function into the highlighted cell. □

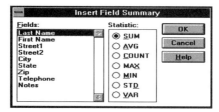

Figure 9.6   The Insert Field Summary dialog box lets you add calculations to your database reports.

You can also construct your own formulas, using field names along with standard arithmetic operators. For example, in an accounts receivable database with fields named "Previous Balance," "Payment," and "New Balance," the instruction =Previous Balance-Payment will calculate the value of New Balance. To add your own formula to a report definition, select the cell in which you want the calculation, type the formula, and then press Enter. The available arithmetic operators are shown in Table 9.1.

FYIdea: Insurance companies can be real sticklers when it comes to documenting losses. Use your database and database reports to create a list of your office or home possessions. Use a formula instruction to calculate the total value of all items in the list. Also, include a description of each item, along with its serial number and other identifying features.

Table 9.1   Arithmetic Operators.

Operator	Function
+	Addition
–	Subtraction
*	Multiplication
/	Division
^	Exponentiation

Changing Column Widths

148

When Works creates a report definition for you, it uses the field widths currently set in the database's List view. You may find that some columns are not wide enough to display the information you want. For example, if you have a Last Name field that's only 15 characters wide, and you have a name that's 17 characters long, you need to change the width of the Last Name field in order to be sure that all the last names in your database are displayed properly. You can easily change the width of a column by placing your mouse pointer on the right edge of the column's button (at the top of the window), holding down the left mouse button, and dragging the edge to the right. To change a column to a precise width, use the following Quick Steps.

 Setting Column Widths

1. Select the column button for the column whose width you want to change.

   Works highlights the column.

2. Select Column Width from the Format pull-down menu.

   The Column Width dialog box appears, as shown in Figure 9.7.

3. Type the new column width.

   The new setting appears in the Width text box.

4. Click on the OK button or press Enter.

   Works sets the column width to its new value.   □

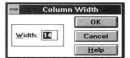

Formats and Alignment

Just as with your database's Form and List views, when creating a report definition, you can set the format in which a field is displayed. You can change the format or alignment of a single cell, or of an entire row or column, by using the appropriate highlighting technique and then choosing a format from the Format pull-down menu, or an alignment from the Toolbar's alignment button.

149

> For more information on setting field formats, alignment, and text attributes, refer to the sections "Setting Field Alignment" and "Setting Field Format" in Chapter 8.

Sorting and Grouping

To make a report truly useful, the data it comprises must be organized in some logical way. Frequently, report data is sorted in numerical or alphabetical order. If you sorted your database before generating your report, the data in the report will also be sorted. However, the Works report generator lets you sort your data into groups, based on the data entered into a specific field. You might, for example, sort an address database on the Last Name field and group entries in your report based on the first letter of the last name. You could also organize groups based on dates, both listing all entries chronologically and grouping them by identical dates.

To sort data into sort breaks while viewing your report definition, select Sort Records from the Select menu. When the Sort Records dialog box appears, type the first field you want used in the sort, and then choose the Ascending or Descending order option button. If you want to create a sort break on the selected field, choose the field's Break option box. If you also want the field sorted by the first letter of the field, select the field's 1st Letter option box. Repeat these steps for the 2nd and 3rd fields, if necessary. When you're finished, click on the OK button or press Enter.

Use the following Quick Steps to sort your database and set up sort breaks.

 Sorting with Sort Breaks

1. While viewing your report definition, select Sort Records from the Select pull-down menu.

   The Sort Records dialog box appears, as shown in Figure 9.8.

2. Type the first field you want used in the sort.

   The field name appears in the 1st Field text box.

3. Choose Ascend A or Descend B order.

   Works highlights the chosen button.

4. If you want to create a sort break on this field, select the Break option box for this field.

   Works places an X in the box, marking it as selected.

5. If you want the sort break based on the first letter of the field, select the 1st Letter option box for this group.

   Works places an X in the box, indicating that the option is selected.

6. If you want your data sorted on more than one field, repeat steps 2 through 5 for the 2nd and 3rd fields.

   Works marks the options you select.

7. Click on the OK button or press Enter.

   Works removes the dialog box from the screen. □

Sort into groups

Sort groups using the
first letter of each entry

*Figure 9.8   The Sort Records dialog box lets you sort
records into groups.*

Works doesn't sort the records until you go to Print preview or
try to print the report. Then it takes your report definition and
applies it, forming the report itself and sending it to the printer or
your screen.

> **Note:** If you don't select the 1st Letter option when setting
> up a sort break, the records are grouped by identical
> entries. For example, in a customer list, all the Smiths would be
> placed in a single group, as would all the Andersons, and so on.

151

Report Querying

There may be times when you want to print only specific records in
your database report. For example, in an inventory database, you
may want to include only those items in the Toy department. To
specify exactly what records to include in a report, you can use the
database query function by selecting the query button, and then
entering the appropriate query instructions into the query form.
After applying the query, only those records that match the query
criteria will appear in the report.

> To learn more about database queries, please refer to the
> section "Basic Database Querying" in Chapter 8.

Renaming Reports

Works allows you to define and save up to four different report definitions for each database. Obviously, you must have a way to tell one report from another. When you first create a report, Works gives it a default name like REPORT1. Because the default names describe reports poorly, Works allows you to enter your own names, up to 15 characters long, using the following Quick Steps.

Renaming a Report

1. Select Name Report from the View pull-down menu.

   The Name Report dialog box appears, as shown in Figure 9.9.

2. In the Reports list box, select the report you want to rename.

   Works highlights the selection.

3. Select the Name text box.

   The blinking text cursor appears in the box.

4. Type the new report name.

   The name appears in the Name text box.

5. Select the Rename button.

   The new name replaces the old name in the Reports list box.

6. Click the OK button or press Enter.

   Works removes the Name Report dialog box and renames the selected report definition. ☐

Figure 9.9   Use the Name Report dialog box to rename report definitions.

Deleting Reports

As we mentioned above, Works allows you to have only four report definitions for each database. This means that you may need to delete a report in order to use its slot for a new one. To delete a report, select Delete Report from the View pull-down menu. When the Delete Report dialog box appears, in the Reports list box, click on the report you want to delete. Next, select the Delete button. Works removes the report from the Reports list box. Click on the OK button or press Enter.

Use the following Quick Steps to delete a report.

 Deleting a Report

1. Select Delete Report from the View pull-down menu.

   The Delete Report dialog box appears, as shown in Figure 9.10.

2. In the Reports list box, select the report you want to delete.

   Works highlights the selected report.

3. Select the Delete button.

   Works removes the report from the Reports list box.

4. Click on the OK button or press Enter.

   Works removes the Delete Report dialog box from the screen, and deletes the report definition from the database's report list.

Figure 9.10   Use the Delete Report dialog box to delete old report definitions.

153

What You Have Learned

- ▶ By using the Create New Report function, you can create a simple report quickly. To access this function, select Create New Report from the View pull-down menu.
- ▶ A report definition is comprised of Title rows, Heading rows, Record rows, Intr rows, Summ rows, and Summary rows, each of which contains report instructions.
- ▶ You can add a row to a report definition by selecting Insert Row/Column from the Edit pull-down menu.
- ▶ You can add text to a report by selecting a cell, and then typing the text.
- ▶ Report instructions tell the report generator where to print data.
- ▶ You can change the column width of a report definition by dragging the right edge of the column's button with your mouse pointer.
- ▶ You can use formatting, alignment, and text attributes in your reports, just as you can in your database's Form and List views.
- ▶ Sort breaks allow you to break a report's data into logical groups.
- ▶ Using the query function, you can limit the records included in a report.

Spreadsheet Basics

In This Chapter

▶ *Understanding cells, text, values, and formulas*
▶ *The spreadsheet screen*
▶ *Viewing a spreadsheet*
▶ *Entering text, number values, formulas, dates, and times*
▶ *Understanding cell references*
▶ *Editing cells*
▶ *Printing a spreadsheet*

Because spreadsheets can perform sophisticated calculations automatically, they are valuable tools for organizing and displaying number-intensive reports. Whenever you change a value in a spreadsheet, it recalculates and redisplays all related values. This not only lets you design reports quickly, but also allows you to experiment with different values, trying "what if" scenarios.

In this chapter, you'll learn to set up a basic spreadsheet, including how to enter values, text, and formulas. You'll also learn to write cell references, enter dates and times, print a spreadsheet, and more.

> **FYIdea:** You can use a spreadsheet for more than just creating reports. You can also use them to create automatic recalculating forms, such as invoices and packing lists.

Cells, Text, Values, and Formulas

A spreadsheet comprises several elements that work together to create documents and reports. These elements are *cells, text strings, values,* and *formulas.* A cell is a specific location in a spreadsheet, identified by its column and row. Columns in a spreadsheet are labeled with letters, and rows with numbers. The intersection of any column and row is a cell. So, cells are identified with the column and row name. For example, the cell at the intersection of column C and row 5 is C5. Each cell can hold a line of text, a value, or a formula.

Text is used to title and label the contents of a spreadsheet. You also use text to add notes or other explanatory items. Values can be numbers, dates, or times. A number value never changes, unless you change it manually. The number displayed by a formula, however, changes whenever the values on which it is based change. It is formulas that give spreadsheets their power. Dates and times may be recalculating or non-recalculating, depending upon how you enter them. We'll discuss these elements of a spreadsheet in great detail later in this chapter.

The Spreadsheet Screen

When you first start the spreadsheet program, you see the screen shown in Figure 10.1. The Menu bar at the top provides access to all the spreadsheet functions. Under the Menu bar is the Toolbar, which provides quick access to frequently used functions, such as field alignment, cell formats, and the auto-sum and charting functions. (Everything on the Toolbar is also available in the menus.)

Below the Toolbar is the Formula bar, which displays the current cell location and the contents of the cell. Below the Formula bar is the spreadsheet workspace. It is here that your spreadsheet windows appear.

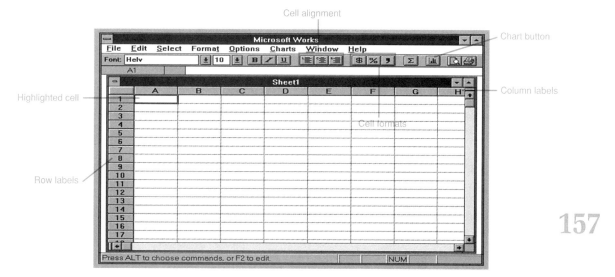

Figure 10.1   The spreadsheet screen.

 To start a new spreadsheet file, refer to the section "Starting a New File" in Chapter 2.

Viewing a Spreadsheet

Works uses grid lines on the screen to separate visually the cells that make up a spreadsheet. There may be times, however, when you don't want the grid lines visible. You can turn off the grid lines by selecting Show Gridlines from the Options pull-down menu, as shown in Figure 10.2. Works then removes the check next to the Show Gridlines entry, showing that the option is off.

Because a spreadsheet can be much larger than your screen, you may need to use the horizontal and vertical scroll bars to view the spreadsheet. When you do this, important row and column titles may no longer be visible, making it difficult to interpret the data displayed on the screen. Luckily, Works can freeze titles so they stay on the screen no matter where you are in your spreadsheet. To freeze column and row titles, select the cell below the row you want to freeze and to the right of the column you want to freeze. Works highlights the cell. Then select Freeze Titles from the Options pull-down menu. Works places a check next to the entry, to show that it is selected, and freezes the selected columns and rows. To unfreeze the titles, select Freeze Titles again. Works removes the check next to the entry and unfreezes the titles.

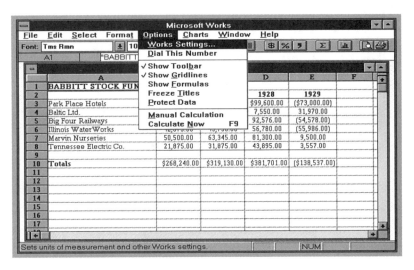

Figure 10.2   Use Show Gridlines from the Options menu to turn the on-screen gridlines on and off. Use the Freeze Titles option to keep titles on-screen as you scroll through a large spreadsheet.

For more information on using window controls to scroll through a spreadsheet, please refer to the section "Viewing a Document" in Chapter 2.

Entering Text

As we said previously, you can enter text into any cell, which gives you the ability to title your spreadsheets, as well as add explanatory notes and labels (see Figure 10.3). To enter text, select the desired cell, type the text, and press Enter. The text appears in the selected cell and also in the Formula bar. You can type up to 255 characters in a text string. If the text is too long to fit in the selected cell, it is displayed on top of the cells to the right if those cells are empty. If the cells to the right contain information, then only the text that will fit in the cell is displayed.

> **Note:** Although a long text string may be displayed on top of more than one cell, it is contained only in the cell in which it was originally typed.

> The text, and other elements, that make up your spreadsheet can be displayed using various alignments and text attributes. Refer to the section "Setting Field Alignment" in Chapter 8 for more information.

Entering Number, Date, and Time Values

Values are numbers, dates, or times that you enter directly into a cell. Number values do not change unless you change them, unlike formulas, which can display different numbers, depending on the contents of the referenced cells. Date and time values also may change, based on your computer's clock.

You enter a number value into a cell just as you enter text by selecting the desired cell, typing the number, and pressing Enter. The number appears in the cell and in the Formula bar. Notice that in the Formula bar, a number is not preceded by a double quote as text strings are.

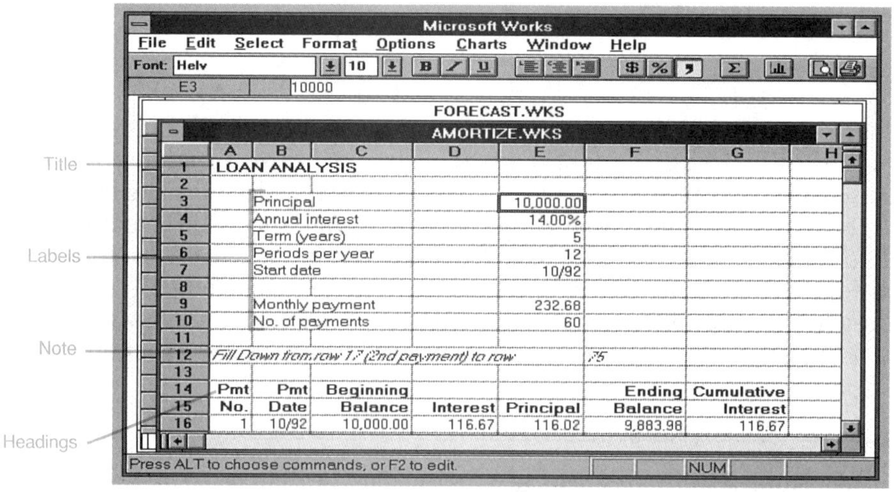

Figure 10.3 You can use text strings to add titles, as well as explanatory notes and labels.

If the number you enter is too long for the cell, Works either displays the number in scientific notation (for example, 3.7E+10) or as the symbol ########, depending on the number's format (see Figure 10.4). If you want to see the full number, you must widen the cell's column.

There are two types of date and time values: *recalculating* and *nonrecalculating.* Unlike number values, which change only if you change them manually, recalculating date and time values may change when a spreadsheet is recalculated.

Dates and times can be displayed in many formats, which are shown in Table 10.1.

Table 10.1 Date and Time Formats.

Long Month/Day/Year	(Jan 21, 1991)
Long Month/Year	(Jan 1991)
Long Month, Day	(Jan 21)
Long Month	(Jan)
Short Month/Day/Year	(01/21/91)
Short Month/Year	(01/91)
Short Month/Day	(01/21)

24-hour Hour/Minute/Second	(15:23:10)
24-hour Hour/Minute	(15:23)
12-hour Hour/Minute/Second	(3:23:10 PM)
12-hour Hour/Minute	(3:23 PM)

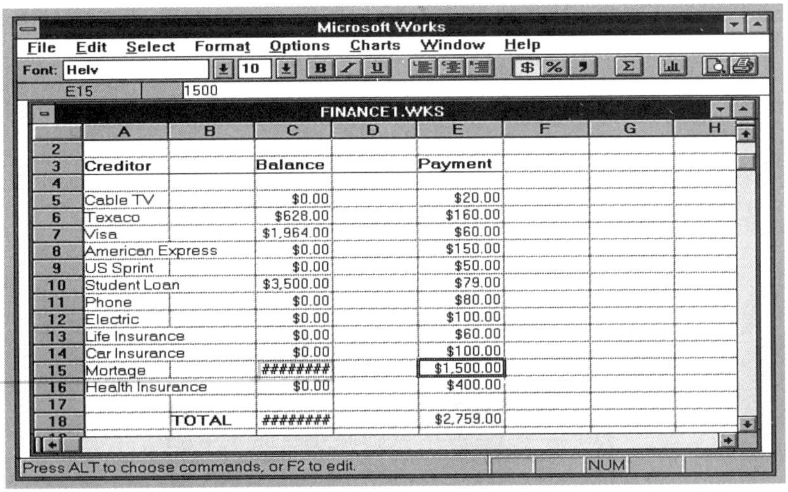

![Microsoft Works screenshot]

The number is too big for the cell

161

Figure 10.4 A number too long for its cell may be displayed as a row of pound signs.

To enter a time or date value, select the desired cell, type the value in one of the formats shown in Table 10.1, and then press Enter. If the time or date you enter is too long to fit into the cell, Works displays the symbol #########. You must then use a shorter version of the time or date, or widen the column.

Recalculating time and date values change automatically whenever Works recalculates the spreadsheet. By using these values, you can always be sure that you've got the current date and time in your spreadsheet. To insert a recalculating date or time, use the following Quick Steps.

Entering Recalculating Times and Dates

1. Select the desired cell.

   Works highlights the cell.

2. Type the formula =NOW( ) and press Enter.

   Works inserts a "raw" time/date value into the cell.

3. Select Time/Date from the Format pull-down menu.

The Time/Date dialog box appears, as shown in Figure 10.5.

4. In the Show group box, select the desired time or date format.

Works marks the selected format.

5. If you chose a date format in the Date group box, select either the Long or Short format option. If you chose a time format in the Time option box, select the 24-hour or 12-hour format button.

Works marks the selected option.

6. Click on the OK button or press Enter.

Works formats the raw time and date to the format you selected.

162

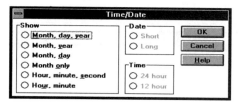

Figure 10.5   The Time/Date dialog box helps you enter recalculating times and dates.

You can use dates and times in calculations, just like any other value. For example, you can subtract one date from another in order to determine how much time passed between them. You can use times similarly.

> **Note:** A time or date entered manually into a cell is a *non-recalculating* value. That is, it changes only when you manually edit it.

> **Tip:** To enter the current time or date value quickly, select the desired cell, and then press Ctrl+semicolon for the date, or Ctrl+Shift+semicolon for the time.

Entering Cell References

Cells are named according to their column and row. For example, the cell at the intersection of column C and row 6 is called C6. You can use cell references in other cells, especially within formulas, referring to them individually, in a list, or in a range. A single reference includes only the cell's name, such as A6. A cell list is a list of single references separated by commas, such as A6,B6,D6,F6. Range references let you refer to a contiguous list of cells by listing only the beginning and ending of the range, separated by a colon. For example, the range reference A4:A7 refers to cells A4, A5, A6, and A7. Examples of each type of reference used in formulas are shown in Table 10.2.

Table 10.2   Cell Reference Types.

Reference	Example
Single	=C5*C6
List	=SUM(B4,B6,B8)
Range	=AVG(A6:A10)

Entering Formulas

While entering numbers, dates, times, and text are all important in the creation of a spreadsheet document, a spreadsheet's power lies in its use of formulas to calculate values for specific cells. Formulas may be little more than cell references (for example, B4, A6, and so on) combined with arithmetic operators, or they may make use of Works' built-in functions, including SUM( ), ABS( ), AVG( ), COUNT( ), LOG( ), and many others.

When you enter a formula into a cell, the value displayed depends upon the values referenced in the formula. For example, if you enter a formula like =B4+G2 into cell C5, Works takes the values in B4 and G2, adds them, and displays the sum in C5. The formula itself is shown only in the Formula bar (unless you have the Show Formulas option selected).

Formulas always start with an equal sign (=), and can include operators, numbers, cell references, and functions. The arithmetic operators supported by the Works spreadsheet are listed in Table 10.3 (in order of precedence). Some of Works' functions are listed in Table 10.4.

Table 10.3   Arithmetic Operators for Spreadsheets.

Operator	Function
^	Exponentiation
–	Negative
+	Positive
*	Multiplication
/	Division
+	Addition
–	Subtraction
=	Equal
< >	Not Equal
<	Less Than
>	Greater Than
< =	Less Than or Equal To
> =	Greater Than or Equal To
~	Not
		OR
&	AND

Note: The standard mathematical rules of precedence are followed when Works evaluates your formulas. Make sure your formulas are set up for the right order of evaluation. Use parentheses where necessary to force a specific order of evaluation.

Table 10.4   *Commonly Used Works Functions.*

Function	Operation
ABS(X)	Absolute value
ACOS(X)	Arccosine
ASIN(X)	Arcsine
ATAN(X)	Arctangent
AVG(VAL1,VAL2,...)	Average
COLS(RANGE)	Number of columns
COS(X)	Cosine
COUNT(RANGE1,RANGE2,...)	Number of cells
DATE(YEAR,MONTH,DAY)	Gives date number
DDB(COST,SALVAGE,LIFE,PERIOD)	Depreciation
FV(PAYMENT,RATE,TERM)	Future value
HLOOKUP(VALUE,RANGE,ROW)	Find an entry
INT(X)	Integer of X
IRR(GUESS,RANGE)	Internal rate of return
LN(X)	Natural logarithm
LOG(X)	Base 10 logarithm
MAX(RANGE1,RANGE2,...)	Largest number
MIN(RANGE1,RANGE2,...)	Smallest number
MOD(NUMERATOR,DENOMINATOR)	Get remainder
NOW()	Get date and time number
NPV(RATE,RANGE)	Net present value
PI()	Returns 3.14159
PMT(PRINCIPLE,RATE,TERM)	Periodic payment for loan
PV(PAYMENT,RATE,TERM)	Present value of an annuity
RAND()	Random number
ROUND(X,NUMBEROFPLACES)	Rounds off X
ROWS(RANGE)	Number of rows
SINE(X)	Sine
SLN(COST,SALVAGE,LIFE)	Straight-line depreciation
SQRT(X)	Square root
STD(RANGE1,RANGE2,...)	Standard deviation
SUM(RANGE1,RANGE2,...)	Sum

165

continues

Table 10.4 *continued*

Function	Operation
SYD(COST,SALVAGE,LIFE,PERIOD)	Sum-of-the-years depreciation
TAN(X)	Tangent
VAR(RANGE1,RANGE2,...)	Variance
VLOOPUP(VALUE,RANGE,COLUMN)	Find an entry

To enter a formula, select the cell, type the formula, and press Enter. Works evaluates the formula immediately, displaying the result in the cell and the formula itself in the Formula bar. When you want to use one of Works' built-in functions, you must type the name of the function, and then place the values for the function within parentheses. For example, to sum cells A4, A5, and A6, you'd type SUM(A4:A6) or SUM(A4,A5,A6). The following Quick Steps summarize this process.

Editing Cells

You might want to use a spreadsheet to experiment with different values in order to see how changing them affects other calculations. To do this, you need to be able to change the contents of a cell. To replace a cell entry with a new one, select the cell, type the new entry, and press Enter. Works replaces the old entry with the new one.

If you want to edit an entry without having to replace it, select the cell, click on the Formula bar (or press F2), and then edit the entry in the Formula bar. Use all the standard editing keys, such as Backspace, Delete, and the direction keys. When you edit a cell, Works automatically recalculates the spreadsheet (unless you have Manual Calculation from the Options menu active).

Printing a Spreadsheet

Because spreadsheets are frequently larger than a single page, Works must use special handling during printing. When you print a spreadsheet that's too large to fit on a single page, Works divides the spreadsheet so that you can paste the pages together and thus reconstruct the entire spreadsheet. As always, before printing a document, you should check it with the Print preview function, to be sure the printed pages look the way you expect.

If you like, you can print a specific section of a spreadsheet. To do this, highlight the desired section, and then select Set Print Area from the File pull-down menu (see Figure 10.6). When you print the document, only the area you highlighted is printed.

If you want to keep headers and gridlines in your printed copy, use the following Quick Steps.

167

 Printing Headers and Gridlines

1. Select Page Setup & Margins from the File pull-down menu.	The Page Setup & Margins dialog box appears, as as shown in Figure 10.7.
2. Select the Print Gridlines or Print Row and Column Headers option boxes.	Works places an X in each selected box.
3. Click on the OK button or press Enter.	Works removes the dialog box from the screen.
4. Print the document.	Works includes the headers or gridlines, depending on the options you selected. □

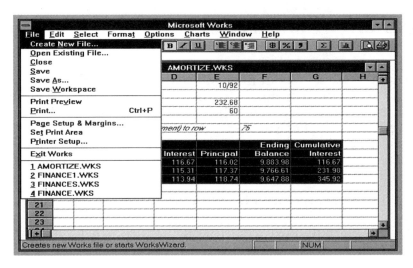

Figure 10.6   To print only a specific section of a spreadsheet, highlight the desired section, and then select Set Print Area from the File menu.

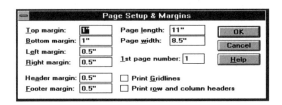

Figure 10.7   You can print headers and gridlines by selecting the appropriate options in the Page Setup & Margins dialog box.

What You Have Learned

▶ A spreadsheet is made up of many cells, which contain text, values, and formulas.

▶ The Formula bar displays the current cell, both its name and its contents.

▶ You can enter recalculating times and dates by using the NOW() function. To enter nonrecalculating times and dates, type them as text.

▶ Cell references can be entered individually, as a list, or as a range.

▶ You create formulas, which always begin with an equal sign, by typing cell references combined with arithmetic operators and functions.

▶ You can print a specific section of a spreadsheet by high-lighting the section, and then selecting Set Print Area from the File menu.

169

Advanced Spreadsheet Functions

In This Chapter

- ► *Selecting, copying, and moving cells*
- ► *Understanding relative and absolute references*
- ► *Changing cell widths*
- ► *Inserting and deleting rows and columns*
- ► *Sorting cell entries*
- ► *Finding specific cells*
- ► *Naming cells and ranges*
- ► *Adding lines and borders*

Now that you know what a spreadsheet is and how to set one up, it's time to look at more advanced spreadsheet functions. In this chapter, you'll learn about highlighting, copying, organizing, naming, and searching for cells. You'll also learn to change cell widths, insert rows and columns, and add borders to your spreadsheet. In addition, we'll talk about relative and absolute references and how they affect the formulas that make up your spreadsheet.

Highlighting Cells

You already know how to highlight a single cell by clicking on it with your mouse pointer. You can also highlight a group of cells, so you can apply a function to many at once (see Figure 11.1). You might do this, for example, to copy or delete a series of cells.

To highlight an entire row, select the row's number (on the left side of the window). To highlight an entire column, select the column's letter button (on the top of the window). To highlight the entire spreadsheet, select the button above row 1 and to the left of column A.

To highlight cells with your keyboard, press F8, and then use the direction keys to move the text cursor over the cells you want to highlight.

You can also highlight a portion of a spreadsheet by placing your mouse pointer on the upper left cell of the group, holding down the left mouse button, and dragging the mouse pointer down to the lower right cell of the group. When you release the mouse button, the selected cells remain highlighted. To turn off highlighting, click anywhere on the spreadsheet or press Escape.

172

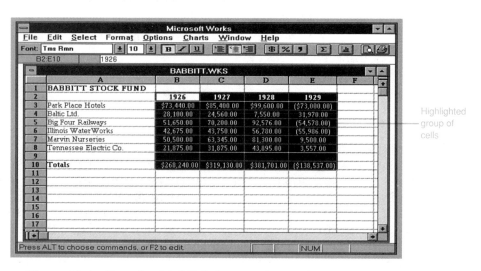

Highlighted group of cells

Figure 11.1   By using highlighting, you can select a group of cells.

Copying and Moving Cells

Often, you'll want to copy information from one group of cells to another. Doing this can save you a lot of extra typing. You might, for example, have several columns that need the same starting values or formulas. To copy cells, highlight the desired cells, and then select Copy from the Edit menu or press Ctrl+C (see Figure 11.2). Works then moves the contents of the cells into the clipboard. After copying the cells into the clipboard, you can paste a copy anywhere in your spreadsheet by selecting the upper left corner of the target group, and selecting Paste from the Edit menu or pressing Shift+V. Works places a copy of the cells in the selected location. You can repeat the Paste function as often as you like.

If you want to copy a cell or group of cells to an adjacent row or column, highlight the cells from which to copy and the cells into which to copy them. (Highlight both rows or columns as a single block.) Then select Fill Right or Fill Down from the Edit menu. Works automatically copies the information into the target cells.

You can move a cell, or a group of cells, by highlighting the desired cells, and then selecting Cut from the Edit menu or pressing Ctrl+X. Works then removes the highlighted cells from the screen and places them into the clipboard, from which they can be pasted in a new location.

Edit functions

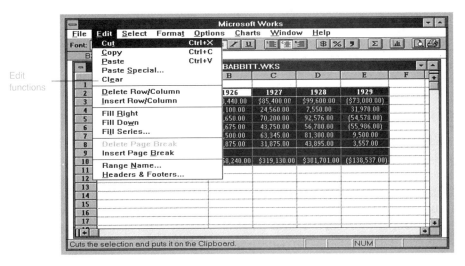

Figure 11.2   The Edit menu provides functions for copying, cutting, and pasting cells or groups of cells.

Relative and Absolute References

You've probably noticed that if you move a group of cells containing formulas, the formulas automatically change so the group still functions properly as a unit. For example, suppose you've entered a formula like =B3 into cell C4. If you move the contents of C4 to D4, one column to the right, the formula changes to =C3. This is because the formula uses *relative referencing*. The formula tells Works to get the value from the cell one column to the left and one row up, rather than to get the contents of B3. When you move the formula in C4 to D4, Works still looks for the value one column to the left and one row up, this time in cell C3. In order for the relative reference to work properly, you also must move B3 along with C4.

There may be times when you don't want to use relative referencing, when you want the formula to use the same cell no matter where you move the formula. You can do this by using *absolute references*. With absolute referencing, the formula =B3 in cell C4 will not change when it is moved. To tell Works that you want to use absolute referencing, you must precede the cell reference in the formula with a dollar sign ($). Moreover, you must use a dollar sign in front of both the row and the column reference. So, our original example formula would be =B3 when using absolute references.

> **Tip:** You can combine relative and absolute references by using a dollar sign in front of only the row or column portion of the cell reference (for example, =B$3 or =$B3).

Changing Cell Width

When Works first starts a new spreadsheet, it sets each column to the default width of 10 characters. Often, you'll want wider columns to display longer numbers or text. You can change a column's width in one of two ways. The easiest method is to place your mouse pointer on the right edge of the column's letter button (at the top of the window), hold down the left mouse button, and drag the edge to the right. If you want to set a column's width to an exact value, place the cursor in the column, and then select Column <u>W</u>idth from the Format menu. The Column Width dialog box appears, into which you can type the required width (see Figure 11.3). When you click on the OK button or press Enter, Works resets the selected column's width.

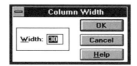

Figure 11.3   The Column Width dialog box lets you set a column's width to an exact measurement.

Inserting Rows and Columns

As you design your spreadsheet, you'll often need to add information between already existing rows and columns. Works allows you to add new rows or columns anywhere in a spreadsheet. To add a row or column, use the following Quick Steps.

 Adding a Row or Column

1. Select the cell where you want the row or column added.

   Works highlights the cell.

2. Select <u>I</u>nsert Row/Column from the Edit pull-down menu (see Figure 11.4).

   The Insert dialog box appears.

3. Select the <u>R</u>ow or <u>C</u>olumn option button.

   Works marks the selected button.

4. Click on the OK button or press Enter.

   Works inserts the new row or column.   □

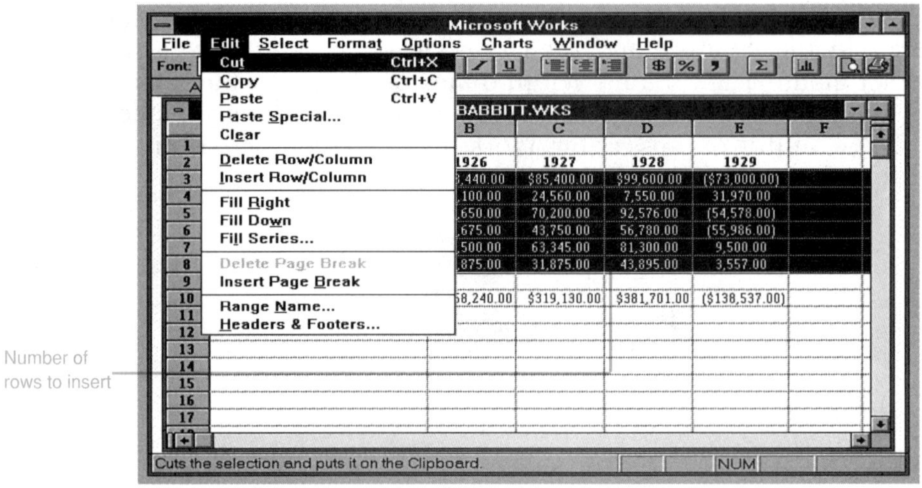

Figure 11.4   To insert multiple new columns or rows,
highlight on the screen the number of columns or rows you
want to add, and then select Insert Row/Column from the
Edit menu.

Deleting Columns and Rows

To close up space between cells, you can delete rows and columns.
To delete a row or column, use the following Quick Steps.

Deleting a Row or Column

1. Select a cell in the desired row or column.

   Works highlights the chosen cell.

2. Select Delete Row/Column from the Edit pull-down menu.

   The Delete dialog box appears.

3. Select the Row or Column option button.

   Works marks the chosen button.

4. Click on the OK button or press Enter.

   Works deletes the selected row or column.

> **Warning:** If you highlight an entire row or column when adding or deleting, Works doesn't display the Insert or Delete dialog box. It just goes ahead and deletes the highlighted row or column.

Sorting Cell Entries

In large spreadsheets with long columns, it's usually helpful to organize your data in alphabetical or numerical order. Works can do this for you. For example, in an inventory list, you could have Works organize your cells by sorting the part names in alphabetical order, or by sorting the part numbers in numerical order, whichever is most convenient. To sort a group of cells, first highlight the columns that contain the data to sort. Then, choose Sort Rows from the Select menu. When the Sort Rows dialog box appears, type the letter of the column that contains the data to sort. If you want to sort the data in more than one column, type the column letters into the 2nd Column and 3rd Column text boxes. Finally, click on the OK button or press Enter. Works sorts the selected rows.

177

Use the following Quick Steps to sort a group of rows.

 Sorting Cells

1. Highlight the columns that contain the data to sort.	Works marks the cells as selected.
2. Choose Sort Rows from the Select pull-down menu.	The Sort Rows dialog box appears, as shown in Figure 11.5.
3. Type the letter of the column that contains the data to sort.	The column letter appears in the 1st Column text box.
4. If you want to sort the data in more than one column, type the column letters into the 2nd Column and 3rd Column text boxes.	The column letters appear in their appropriate text boxes.
5. Click on the OK button or press Enter.	Works sorts the selected rows.

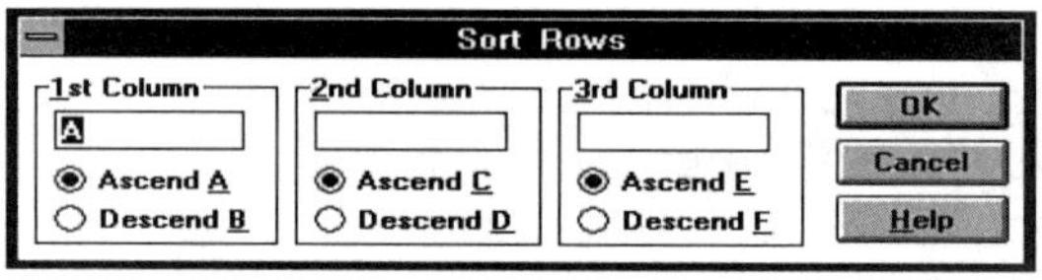

Figure 11.5   Using the Sort function, you can arrange spreadsheet entries into alphabetical or numerical order.

Searching for Specific Cells

Sometimes you may want to jump quickly to a specific location in a large spreadsheet. You can do this by using the spreadsheet's Search function to locate a cell in a highlighted section, or in an entire spreadsheet. The following Quick Steps detail how to use the Search function.

178

Searching for a Specific Cell

1. If you want to search only a section of your spreadsheet, highlight the cells through which you want to search.

   Works marks the cells as selected.

2. If you want to search an entire spreadsheet, leave the spreadsheet unhighlighted.

   Works then knows it should search the entire spreadsheet.

3. Choose Find from the Select pull-down menu.

   The Find dialog box appears, as shown in Figure 11.6.

4. Type the item you want to find.

   What you type appears in the Find What text box.

5. Select the Rows option button if you want to search left to right through rows. Select the Columns button if you want to search top to bottom through columns.

   Works marks the selected button.

6. Click on the OK button or press Enter.

   Works finds the first occurrence of the item and highlights it.

Figure 11.6   The Find dialog box appears when you choose Find from the Select menu.

Tip: If you're not sure of an entry's spelling, you can use wild cards (? and *) to make a search easier. Use a ? in place of an unknown letter (for example, SM?TH to find SMITH or SMYTH). Use the * to replace more than one character (for example, SM*H to find SMITH, SMYTH, or any name that starts with SM and ends with H).

Naming Cells and Ranges

In a complex spreadsheet, formulas like C12-C13 can be cryptic. You can waste a lot of time searching through your worksheet to find the right cell references. To solve this problem, Works allows you to name cells so you can have formulas like BALANCE-PAYMENT, which are much easier to read and understand. You can, in fact, name not only individual cells, but also an entire range of cells. Use the following Quick Steps to name cells and ranges.

 Naming Cells and Ranges

1. Highlight the cell or range of cells you want to name.

   Works marks the cells as selected.

2. Select Range Name from the Edit pull-down menu.

   The Range Name dialog box appears, as sown in Figure 11.7.

3. Type a name for the cell or range.

   The name appears in the Name text box.

4. Click on the OK button or press Enter.

   Works names the selected cell or range.

After naming a cell or range, you can use the name as you would use any cell reference.

For example, let's say we have a spreadsheet in which cell C4 is a customer's monthly payment, and C5 is the customer's previous balance. Now, we want to have the customer's new balance in cell C6. We could just type the formula =C5-C4. But a better idea would be to name cell C4 BALANCE and name cell C5 PAYMENT. Then, we could write our formula as =BALANCE-PAYMENT, which not only performs the calculation, but also shows what we're doing.

To delete a name, select Range Name from the Edit menu, select the name to delete in the Names list box, and select the Delete button. To exit the dialog box without having to rename the cell or range, click on the Cancel button.

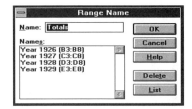

Figure 11.7   The Range Name dialog box lets you name cells or ranges so they're easier to use in formulas.

Adding Borders

To help organize your data into a more readable form, you can add borders and lines to your spreadsheet (see Figure 11.8). By combining many cell borders, you can even create boxes, which you can use to group visually related data. To add a border, use the following Quick Steps.

 Adding Lines and Borders

1. Highlight the cells to which you want to add borders.

   Works marks the cells as selected.

2. Select Border from the Format pull-down menu.

   The Border dialog box appears.

3. If you want to enclose the highlighted cells in a box, select the Outline button. Otherwise, select the Top, Bottom, Left, or Right buttons (you can choose more than one).

    Works marks the buttons as selected.

4. Click on the OK button or press Enter.

    Works adds the selected borders.

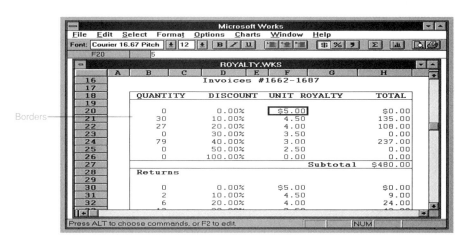

Figure 11.8   Cell borders help visually organize your spreadsheet data.

181

To delete cell borders, highlight the desired cells, select Border from the Format menu, choose the appropriate buttons, and click on the OK button. Works removes the selected borders.

What You Have Learned

▶ You can highlight an entire row of cells, an entire column of cells, or any group of cells, by selecting the row or column buttons or by using the click and drag method.

▶ You can cut, copy, and paste cells by using the edit functions available in the Edit pull-down menu.

▶ A formula that uses relative references changes when it is moved. A formula that uses absolute references doesn't change when moved.

▶ You can insert or delete rows and columns by using the Insert and Delete functions found in the Edit pull-down menu.

▶ You can name cells or ranges to make them easier to use in formulas.

▶ Borders help visually organize your spreadsheet's data.

182

Charting

In This Chapter

- ► *Creating simple charts*
- ► *Managing chart files*
- ► *Chart types*
- ► *Chart modifications and enhancements*
- ► *Adding grids and borders*
- ► *Printing a chart*

Although spreadsheets allow you to display numerical data in report form, there may be times when you'd like to have something more visual. Therefore, Works includes a charting program that lets you display data from your spreadsheets in chart form. Charts are perfectly suited for summarizing data or for determining trends. In this chapter, you'll learn to create charts and how to modify them to fit your needs.

Simple Charting

Works can automatically create a simple bar chart from the data you select, as shown in Figure 12.1. Once you have the bar chart made, you can modify it further to fit specific needs. To create a simple chart, highlight the cells that contain the desired data, and then click on the Chart button from the Toolbar. Or, you can select Create New Chart from the Charts pull-down menu. Works creates the chart, using the values you highlighted. If you also highlight column or row labels in your spreadsheet, Works uses them as labels for the chart.

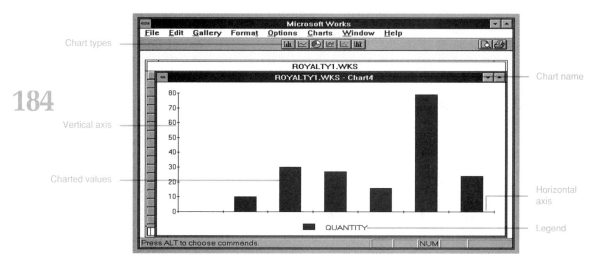

Figure 12.1   *Works automatically creates simple bar graphs using the data you select.*

The following Quick Steps review this procedure.

 Creating a Simple Chart

1. Highlight the cells that contain the desired data.

    Works marks the cells as selected.

2. Click on the Chart button, or select Create New Chart from the Charts pull-down menu.

    Works creates the chart, using the values you highlighted.

Charting Nonadjacent Values

Because you can highlight only one group of cells at a time, a problem arises when you want to chart values in nonadjacent rows or columns. Luckily, Works allows you to add cell references manually to your chart, so you can chart groups of cells located anywhere in your spreadsheet.

To do this, highlight the first group of cells you want to include in the chart, and click on the Chart button or select Create New Chart from the Charts pull-down menu. Then, select Series from the Edit pull-down menu. When the Series dialog box appears (see Figure 12.2), select the first empty Series text box, and type the cell-range reference for the data you want to add to the chart (for example, C4:C14). Repeat this procedure for other series you want to add. Finally, select the OK button or press Enter.

185

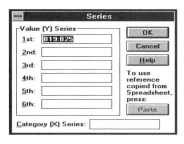

Figure 12.2   The Series dialog box lets you manually enter or delete cell ranges you want to include in a chart.

The following Quick Steps outline the procedure for adding data groups.

 Adding Nonadjacent Data Groups

1. Highlight the first group of cells you want to include in the chart, and click on the Chart button, or select Create New Chart from the Charts pull-down menu.

   Works creates a standard bar chart from the highlighted data.

2. Select Series from the Edit pull-down menu.

   The Series dialog box appears.

3. Select the first empty Series text box.	The text cursor appears in the selected box.
4. Type the cell-range reference for the data you want to add to the chart.	The range reference appears in the selected text box.
5. If you want to add another data group, repeat steps 3 and 4.	The range references appear in the text boxes.
6. Select the OK button or press Enter.	Works updates the chart with the new data. □

Saving a Chart

Works allows you to create up to eight different charts for each spreadsheet. To save your charts, you need only save the spreadsheet. The charts are automatically saved along with your spreadsheet data.

 If you need help saving a spreadsheet file, refer to the section "Saving a File" in Chapter 2.

Naming a Chart

When Works first creates a chart, it gives it a generic name, such as "Chart 1." You can change the chart names to more descriptive names. For example, you might want to give a chart that illustrates monthly profits the name "Profits."

To name a chart, select Name from the Charts pull-down menu. When the Name Chart dialog box appears, shown in Figure 12.3, select the chart you want to name. Then, select the Name text box, or press the Tab key. Type the chart's new name, select the Rename button, and select the OK button or press Enter.

Figure 12.3   Use the Name dialog box to rename spread-sheet charts.

The following Quick Steps detail this procedure.

 Naming a Chart

1. Select Name from the   The Name Chart dialog box
   Charts pull-down menu.   appears.

2. In the Charts list box,   Works highlights the chart's
   select the chart you want   name.
   to name.

3. Select the Name text box,   The text cursor appears in
   or press the Tab key.   the Name text box.

4. Type the chart's new   The name appears in the
   name.   Name text box.

5. Select the Rename button.   Works renames the selected
                                 chart.

6. Select the OK button or   Works removes the dialog
   press Enter.   box from the screen.   ☐

187

Viewing a Chart

When Works creates a new chart, it gives the chart its own window
and adds the chart's name to both the Chart and Window pull-down
menus. The entry on the Chart menu remains until you delete the
chart. The entry on the Window menu stays only as long as the
chart's window is open.

You can view any open chart window by selecting the chart's
name in the Window pull-down menu. If a chart is not yet opened,
you can open it by selecting the chart's name in the Charts pull-down

menu (see Figure 12.4). To get back to your spreadsheet window, select the spreadsheet's name in the Window menu.

Once a chart is open, you can resize its window, just like any other window. Works enlarges or reduces the size of the graph to fit the window.

 For information about using window controls, refer to the section "Navigating the Works Document Window" in Chapter 2.

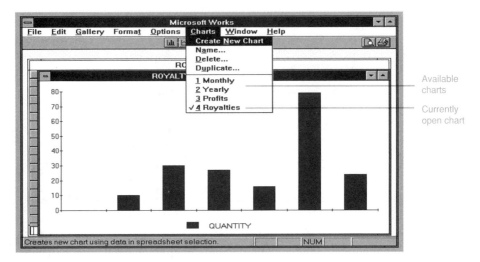

Figure 12.4 You can open an existing chart by selecting its name in the Charts pull-down menu.

Changing a Chart's Type

Although Works first creates your chart in bar-chart form, you can change the chart to a different type. There are six basic types from which to choose, each offering several variations of the chosen chart type (see Figure 12.5).

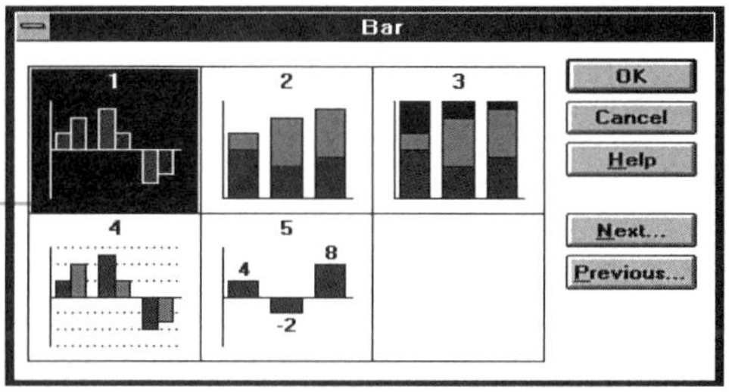

Figure 12.5   Works can display the six basic chart types in a variety of ways.

The following list details the six basic chart types.

Bar Chart: In a bar chart, values are represented by bars. The higher the bar, the higher the value. This type of chart lets you easily compare data.

Line Charts: Line charts are formed by first plotting each value on the chart, and then connecting the plotted points with lines. This type of chart lets you easily see trends over time.

189

Pie Charts: The values in a pie chart are shown as "slices" of a circle, allowing you to more easily judge proportions.

Stacked Line Charts: This type of chart is like many line charts stacked on top of each other, and lets you compare trends of several groups of data.

Scatter Charts: Scatter charts take two or more groups of related data and plot them, placing related values in the same Y position. This type of chart allows you to compare related data.

Combination Charts: Combination charts let you use bar graphs and line graphs on the same chart, which is another way to compare related groups of data.

To change a chart's type, use the following Quick Steps.

Changing a Chart's Type

1. Open the chart's window and select one of the chart-type buttons on the Toolbar, or select the chart type from the Gallery pull-down menu.

Works displays the chart dialog box.

2. Each chart type can be displayed in several ways. To choose the display option, select the desired chart figure.	Works highlights the selected figure.
3. Select the OK button or press Enter.	Works displays your chart in the new format. □

Adding Chart Titles

After generating your chart, you'll probably want to dress it up a little by adding titles and other text elements. You can, for example, not only add a title to the top of your chart, but also to the horizontal and vertical axes. To add titles to your chart, select <u>T</u>itles from the Edit pull-down menu. The Titles dialog box appears (see Figure 12.6). Type whatever titles you want to add into the appropriate text boxes, and then select the OK button or press Enter. Works adds the titles to your chart.

To delete a chart title, call up the Titles dialog box, and remove the title from the text box.

Figure 12.6   Use the Titles dialog box to add several types of titles to a chart.

Adding Category Labels

To make a chart more understandable, you may want to add category labels, as shown in Figure 12.7, which Works places just below the chart on the horizontal axis. For example, if you had a chart showing profit growth over the course of a year, you'd probably want to have category labels marking each month in the chart.

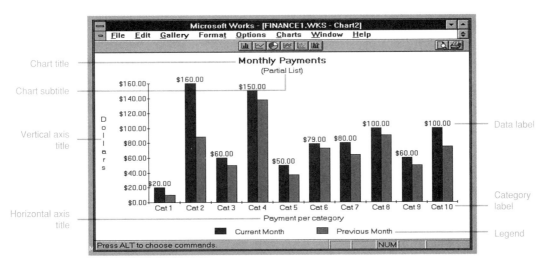

Figure 12.7   *You can add various types of labels to your charts.*

You can add category labels by typing them into the spreadsheet, copying them to the clipboard, and then pasting them into the chart.

To add category labels, first switch to or open your spreadsheet's window, and type the desired category labels into the spreadsheet, one to a cell. Then, highlight the labels, and copy them by selecting Copy from the Edit pull-down menu, or by pressing Ctrl+C. Switch to or open the chart's window, and select Paste Series from the Edit menu, or press Ctrl+V. When the Paste Series dialog box appears (see Figure 12.8), select the Category option in the Use Selection group box. Finally, select the OK button or press Enter.

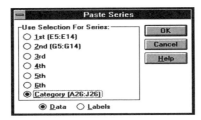

Figure 12.8   *The Paste Series dialog box lets you add category labels to your charts.*

The following Quick Steps illustrate this procedure.

 Adding Category Labels

1. Switch to or open your spreadsheet's window.

   Works displays your spreadsheet in the active window.

2. Type the desired category labels into the spreadsheet, one to a cell.

   The label text appears in the spreadsheet.

3. Highlight the labels, and then copy them by selecting Copy from the Edit pull-down menu, or by pressing Ctrl+C.

   Works copies the labels into the clipboard.

4. Switch to or open the chart's window.

   Works displays the chart in the active window.

5. Select Paste Series from the Edit menu, or press Ctrl+V.

   The Paste Series dialog box appears.

6. Select the Category option in the Use Selection group box.

   Works marks the button as selected.

7. Select the OK button or press Enter.

   Works adds the new category labels to your chart. □

To delete category labels, switch to the chart window, select Series in the Edit menu, and delete the contents of the Category (X) Series box. Then select the OK button or press Enter. Works removes the labels from the chart.

You can change the "frequency" of category labels (how many columns between labels), by selecting Horizontal (X) Axis from the Format pull-down menu, and typing a new number into the Label Frequency dialog box.

Adding Data Labels

Data labels are another type of label you can add to bar, line, and pie charts. In a bar or line chart, Works places data labels above the appropriate bars or points. In a pie chart, Works places data labels next to each pie slice. Pie charts can have two labels for each pie slice, as shown in Figure 12.9a.

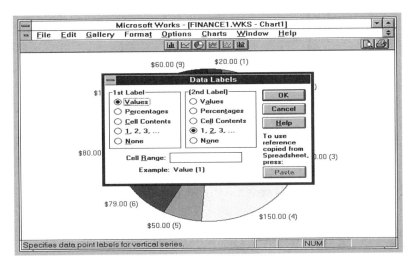

Figure 12.9a   Pie charts can have two types of data labels for each slice.

You can choose from the types shown in Table 12.1.

Table 12.1   Data Label Types for Pie Charts.

Type	Description
Values	Show the values upon which the slice is based.
Percentages	Show the sizes of the slice as compared to the whole.
Cell Contents	Show the content of cell ranges you specify.
1,2,3	Numbers the slices sequentially.
None	Shows no label.

To add data labels to a pie chart, open the chart's window and select <u>D</u>ata Labels from the Edit pull-down menu. When the Data Labels dialog box appears (see Figure 12.9b), select the desired label types in the 1st Label and 2nd Label group boxes, and select the OK button or press Enter. Works adds the labels to the chart. To delete data labels, select the None button in the Data Labels dialog box.

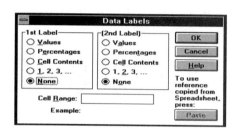

Figure 12.9b   The Data Labels dialog box lets you add data labels to your charts.

194

To add data labels to a bar chart, type them into the spreadsheet, copy them to the clipboard, and then paste them into the chart. The following Quick Steps review this procedure.

Adding Data Labels to a Line or Bar Chart

1. Open your spreadsheet's window.

   Works displays your spreadsheet in the active window.

2. Type the desired data labels into the spreadsheet, one to a cell.

   The label text appears in the spreadsheet.

3. Highlight the labels, and then copy them by selecting <u>C</u>opy from the Edit pull-down menu, or by pressing Ctrl+C.

   Works copies the labels into the clipboard.

4. Open the chart's window.

   Works displays the chart in the active window.

5. Select <u>D</u>ata Labels from the Edit menu.

   The Data Labels dialog box appears.

6. In the Value (Y) Series group box, select the series where you want the labels placed.	The text cursor appears in the selected box.
7. Select the Paste button.	Works places the labels' cell reference in the selected series box.
8. Select the OK button or press Enter.	Works adds the new data labels to your chart. ☐

To delete data labels from a line or bar chart, open the chart, select Data Labels in the Edit menu, delete the appropriate ranges from the Value (Y) Series text boxes, and then select the OK button or press Enter. Works removes the selected data labels from the chart.

> **Tip:** By using the actual values for each category as labels on your chart, you can show both the relationship between the values (by comparing the bars), as well as see the exact values without having to judge them from the size of the bar.

Changing the Scale of the Vertical Axis

When it first creates a report, Works automatically calculates a scale for the vertical axis by assuming you want the scale to start at zero and that you want to use the largest data value as the high end of the scale. You might, however, want to change these values to ones that better suit a specific case. For example, in a chart illustrating profits over a year, you'd probably want the scale's maximum higher than the maximum profit, so that next year you can use the same scale and show higher profits (you hope). If you use two different scales, it would be difficult to compare the two charts.

To change the scale of the vertical axis, open the chart and select Vertical (Y) Axis from the Format menu. When the Vertical Axis dialog box appears (see Figure 12.10), type in new numbers for the minimum, maximum, and interval values. Then when you select the OK button, Works changes the scale to your specifications.

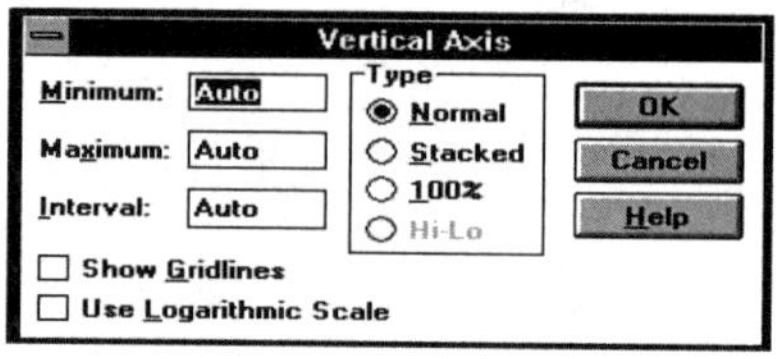

Figure 12.10   The Vertical Axis dialog box allows you to reset the scale used on the vertical axis.

Use the following Quick Steps to change the vertical axis scale.

Changing the Vertical Axis Scale

1. Open the chart.

   Works displays the chart in the active window.

2. Select Vertical (Y) Axis from the Format pull-down menu.

   The Vertical Axis dialog box appears.

3. Type new values into the Minimum, Maximum, and Interval text boxes.

   Works will use these new values to recreate the vertical axis.

4. Select the OK button or press Enter.

   Works closes the dialog box and redraws the chart with the new scale values.

> **Tip:** You can also use the Vertical Axis dialog box to change between standard and logarithmic scales. Works calculates a standard scale by adding the interval to the last value used. It calculates a logarithmic scale by multiplying the last value used by a specific amount, usually 10.

Adding and Editing Legends

In charts that show many related values, it's a good idea to include a legend that describes each value in a category. Legends are printed below the chart and include a label, along with a sample of the bar that represents that value. For example, Figure 12.11 uses a legend to distinguish previous from current month values in the chart. When you first create your report, if you include legend text in the cells from which Works generates the chart, then Works will automatically create the legend for you. You can, however, add your own legends and change or delete existing legends.

To add or edit legends, open the chart window and select Legend from the Edit pull-down menu. The Legend dialog box appears (see Figure 12.11). Add or change the desired legends. To delete a legend, simply delete its entry. When you're done editing, select the OK button or press Enter. Works updates the chart's legend.

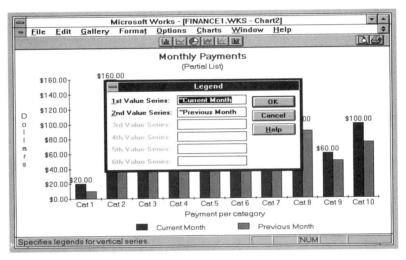

Figure 12.11   The Legend dialog box lets you add a legend to your chart, or edit an existing legend.

Changing Colors, Patterns, and Markers

When Works creates a chart, it automatically uses appropriate colors and patterns. However, you may want to change these settings. For example, certain colors or patterns may not print properly on your printer. You can easily change the patterns and colors in your chart by opening the chart, selecting <u>P</u>atterns & Colors from the Format menu, and changing the color and pattern settings in the dialog box that appears (see Figure 12.12).

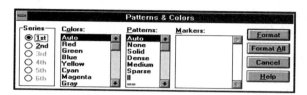

Figure 12.12   Use the Colors & Patterns dialog box to change a chart's colors, patterns, and markers.

The following Quick Steps detail this procedure.

Changing Colors and Patterns

1. Open the desired chart.

   Works displays the selected chart in the active window.

2. Select <u>P</u>atterns & Colors from the Format pull-down menu.

   The Patterns & Colors dialog box appears.

3. In the Series or Slices group box, select the series or pie slice you want to change.

   Works marks the series or slice as selected.

4. In the Colors group box, select the color you want used on the selected series or pie slice.

   Works marks the color as selected.

5. In the Patterns group box, select the pattern you want to use on the selected series or pie slice.

   Works marks the pattern as selected.

6. Select the <u>F</u>ormat button.

   Works sets the color and pattern for the selected series or slice.

7. Repeat steps 3 through 6 for each series or pie slice you want to change.

   Works sets the color and pattern for each of your choices.

8. Select the <u>C</u>lose button.

   Works displays the chart using the new colors and patterns.

On charts using lines or points, you can also use the Colors & Patterns dialog box to change the type of point markers displayed. You can choose from 10 types: filled box, filled circle, filled diamond, asterisk, hollow box, hollow circle, hollow diamond, dot, dash, and none.

> **Tip:** If you're using a pie chart, you can "explode" a pie slice by selecting the slice in the Patterns & Colors dialog box, selecting the Explode Slice option box, and then selecting the Format and Close buttons.

Adding Grids and Borders

199

When creating bar and line charts, you might want to add gridlines to the chart (see Figure 12.13). These lines help to translate the height of a bar or marker into its actual value, by providing references to the values on the vertical and horizontal axes. You might, for example, want to use the grid lines when its important that the values in the chart be interpreted precisely. To add grid lines, open the chart and select the desired axis in the Format pull-down menu. In the dialog box that appears, select the Show Gridlines option box, and then select the OK button or press Enter. Works adds the selected gridlines to the chart.

You can also add a border to your chart by selecting Show Border from the Format pull-down menu. When you select this option, Works places a check next to the option in the menu and draws a border around your chart.

> **Tip:** Making basic charts with Works is so easy, you can make temporary ones to get a quick overview of recently entered data. To save space on your hard disk, delete temporary charts at the end of a Works session.

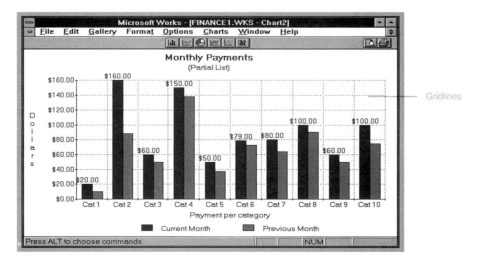

Figure 12.13   Adding grid lines to a chart makes it easier to interpret the data represented.

Deleting Charts

Works allows you to have up to eight charts associated with a spreadsheet file. This is plenty for just about any spreadsheet application. But you may run into situations where you want to delete one or more charts, if for no other reason than unneeded charts unnecessarily increase the size of a spreadsheet file. To delete a report, use the following Quick Steps.

Deleting Charts

1. Select Delete from the Charts pull-down menu.	The Delete Chart dialog box appears (see Figure 12.14).
2. In the Charts list box, select the chart you want to delete.	Works highlights the selected chart.
3. Select the Delete button.	Works removes the selected chart from the Charts list box.

4. Select the OK button or press Enter.

Works closes the dialog box and removes the selected chart from the spread-sheet.

Figure 12.14   You can use the Delete Chart dialog box to remove old charts from a database.

Printing a Chart

Just as with any document, you can send a copy of a chart to your printer. Because charts use graphics rather than just text to display your data, you may have to experiment with different chart colors and patterns to get the printout right. This is especially true if you are using a black-and-white printer. In this case, before printing your chart, select Display As Printed from the Options menu. Your chart then appears on the screen as it will look on the printed page. Remember also, to check Print preview (see Figure 12.15), to make sure your chart is aligned on the page properly.

 To learn more about printing documents, consult Chapter 5.

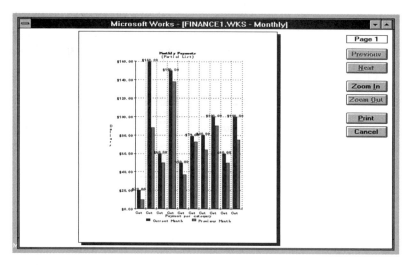

Figure 12.15   Use Print preview to make sure your chart is going to print the way you think.

What You Have Learned

▶ Works can automatically create simple charts.

▶ You can chart nonadjacent spreadsheet values by using the Series function, found in the Edit menu.

▶ When you save a spreadsheet, Works automatically saves any existing charts, too.

▶ By using the Charts and Window menus, you can open charts and switch between windows.

▶ Works allows you to create bar, line, pie, scatter, and combination charts, each of which includes several forms.

▶ You can add titles, labels, and legends to your charts.

▶ You can change any of the colors, patterns, or markers used in a chart.

▶ You can add both gridlines and borders to your charts.

▶ You may have to experiment to get a chart to print exactly as you like.

Sharing Data Between Tools

In This Chapter

▶ *Understanding copied, linked, and embedded objects*
▶ *Copying data into a word processor document*
▶ *Linking data into a word processor document*
▶ *Embedding drawings into a word processor document*
▶ *Sizing, copying, and deleting objects*
▶ *Creating form letters, mailing labels, and envelopes*
▶ *Copying data into a database or spreadsheet*

One advantage of using an integrated package like Works is the ease with which you can share data between tools. For example, if you want to add a quick report to a business letter, you can copy data from a spreadsheet document into the letter. You can even copy a chart from a spreadsheet. Moreover, when you change the data in the spreadsheet, the data in the letter changes too, ensuring that it's always up to date.

Most often, you'll transfer data from the database or spreadsheet into a word processor document, but as you'll see in this chapter, you can share data in several other ways as well.

Copied, Linked, and Embedded Objects

To understand the process by which Works shares data between tools, you must first understand the difference between *copied*, *linked*, and *embedded* objects. Each type of object works differently and yields different results.

A copied object is one that retains no association with the tool that created it. For example, when you copy a table from a word processing document into a spreadsheet, although you can use the copied values in the spreadsheet, the values retain no connection to the original word processing document. A copied object doesn't change when its source data changes.

A linked object, on the other hand, maintains a connection with the tool that created it. When the source data changes, the linked object does too. You create this type of object, for example, when you add a chart from a spreadsheet into a word processing document.

An embedded object has a different type of connection with its creator. When you select an embedded object, the tool that created the object is automatically started and the object loaded into it. After you modify the object, you then paste it back into the target document. An example of an embedded object is a drawing created with Microsoft Draw that you've added into a word processing document.

 Tip: Whenever possible, use linked data in your documents, so you can be sure the documents stay up to date.

The Word Processor and Shared Data

Usually when you copy, link, or embed an object from one tool to another, your destination is the word processor. This is because you usually use charts and tables in letters and reports to present data to other people. Copied (versus linked or embedded) data shared with the word processor becomes a text paragraph in the target document. After you copy the data, you can modify it just like any other text paragraph. Charts, drawings, and *linked* spreadsheet data, however, are added to word processor documents as objects, which retain a connection with the tool that created them.

Copying Database Data

When you copy data from a database into a word processor document, Works does its best to retain the data's format. That is, Works copies the data into the document in table form (see Figure 13.1), placing one record per line, and placing tabs between the fields of each record.

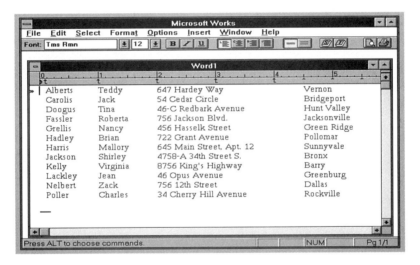

Figure 13.1   Database data is copied into a word processor document in table form.

To copy information from a database, open both the word processor and database documents. When the documents are loaded, switch to the database window and set it to List view. Highlight the records you want to copy, and then select Copy from the Edit menu, or press Ctrl+C. Next, switch to the word processor document window, and place the text cursor where you want the database data copied. Select Paste from the Edit menu, or press Ctrl+V.

The following Quick Steps review this procedure.

Copying Database Data to a Word Processor Document

1. Open the desired word processor and database documents.

   Works loads the documents into windows.

2. Select the database's name in the Window pull-down menu.

   Works switches to the database window.

3. Click on the List View button on the Toolbar, or select List from the View menu.

   Works changes the window to List view.

4. Highlight the records you want to copy.

   Works marks the records as selected.

5. Select Copy from the Edit pull-down menu, or press Ctrl+C.

   Works copies the selected data into the clipboard.

6. Select the word processor document's name in the Window pull-down menu.

   Works switches to the word processor window.

7. Place the text cursor where you want the copied data placed, and then select Paste from the Edit pull-down menu, or press Ctrl+V.

   Works copies the database data into your word processor document.

   □

Copying Spreadsheet Data

You can also copy data, in text form, from a spreadsheet into a word processor document (see Figure 13.2). You might do this, for example, when you want to include a short report along with a business letter. Use a copy when you're not concerned about the letter staying current. When you copy data from a spreadsheet, it is placed into your document in table form, with tabs between the contents of each cell.

To copy data from a spreadsheet, first open both the word processor and spreadsheet documents, and then switch to the spreadsheet window. Highlight the cells you want to copy, and select Copy from the Edit menu, or press Ctrl+C. Next, switch to the word processor document window, and with the text cursor located where you want the data copied, select Paste from the Edit menu, or press Ctrl+V.

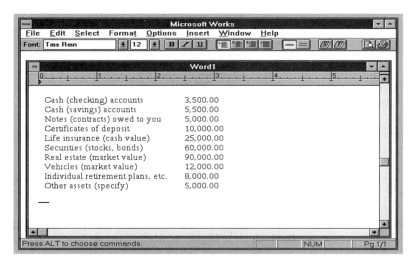

Figure 13.2   Copied spreadsheet data retains no connection with its source data.

The following Quick Steps guide you through this process.

 Copying from a Spreadsheet to a Word Processing Document

1. Open both the word processor and spreadsheet documents.	Works loads each document into a window.
2. Select the spreadsheet's name in the Window pull-down menu.	The spreadsheet window becomes the active window.
3. Highlight the cells you want to copy.	Works marks the cells as selected.
4. Select Copy from the Edit menu, or press Ctrl+C.	Works copies the selected cells into the clipboard.
5. Select the word processor document's name in the Window pull-down menu.	Works switches to the word processor document.

6. With the cursor located where you want the data copied, select Paste from the Edit menu, or press Ctrl+V.

Works copies the spreadsheet data, in table form, into the word processor document. ☐

Linking Spreadsheet Data

If you want to be sure that the spreadsheet data in your word processor document stays current, you should link the data rather than copy it. Then, whenever you change the spreadsheet document, the data in the word processor document is automatically updated.

To link spreadsheet data into a word processor document, open both the word processor and spreadsheet documents. Then, switch to the spreadsheet window, and highlight the cells you want to link. Copy the cells onto the clipboard by selecting Copy from the Edit menu or by pressing Ctrl+C. Now, switch to the word processor window, and with the text cursor located where you want the data copied, select Paste Special from the Edit menu. When the Paste Special dialog box appears, select MS Works Spreadsheet from the Data Type box and then the Paste Link button.

The following Quick Steps offer step-by-step instructions for this procedure.

 Linking Spreadsheet Data to a Word Processing Document

1. Open both the word processor and spreadsheet documents.

Works loads each document into a window.

2. Select the spreadsheet's name in the Window pull-down menu.

Works switches to the spreadsheet window.

3. Highlight the cells you want to link.

Works marks the cells as selected.

4. Select Copy from the Edit menu, or press Ctrl+C.

Works copies the selected cells into the clipboard.

5. Select the word processor document's name in the Window pull-down menu.

Works switches to the word processor document.

6. With the text cursor located where you want the data copied, select Paste Special from the Edit menu.

The Paste Special dialog box appears.

7. In the Data Type list box, select MS Works Spreadsheet.

Works highlights your choice.

8. Select the Paste Link button.

Works copies the spreadsheet data, as a linked object, into the word processing document, as shown in Figure 13.3.   □

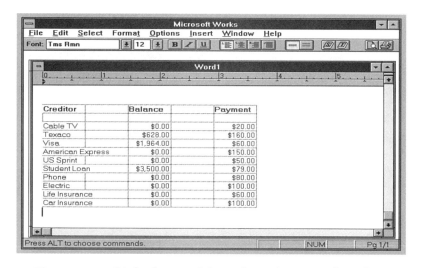

Figure 13.3   Linked spreadsheet data changes when the spreadsheet changes.

Linking a Spreadsheet Chart

Because charts provide a quick way to summarize data and can add a little zip to your word processor documents, you may want to link your spreadsheet data in chart form.

To link a spreadsheet chart, open the word processor document and spreadsheet document containing the desired chart. Then, switch to the word processor window, and with the text cursor placed where you want the chart, select <u>C</u>hart from the Insert pull-down menu. When the Insert Chart dialog box appears, select the spreadsheet containing the chart you want to link in the Spread-sheets list box. Next, in the Charts list box, select the desired chart. Finally, select the OK button or press Enter. The following Quick Steps review this process.

Linking a Spreadsheet Chart to a Word Processor Document

1. Open both the word processor and spreadsheet documents.	Works loads each document into a window.
2. Select the word processor document's name in the Window pull-down menu.	Works switches to the word processor window.
3. With the text cursor placed where you want the chart, select <u>C</u>hart from the Insert pull-down menu.	The Insert Chart dialog box appears.
4. In the Spreadsheets list box, select the spreadsheet that contains the chart you want to link.	Works highlights your selection.
5. In the Charts list box, select the chart you want to link.	Works highlights the selected chart.
6. Select the OK button or press Enter.	Works links the spreadsheet chart into your word processor document, as shown in Figure 13.4.

Embedding a Drawing

Like charts, drawings help spruce up a document (see Figure 13.5). You might, for example, want to create a letterhead using a drawing created with Microsoft Draw. When you embed a drawing into a word processor document, you can edit the drawing anytime by double-clicking on it. Works then starts Microsoft Draw and loads the drawing into it. You make your changes, and then embed it back into your document.

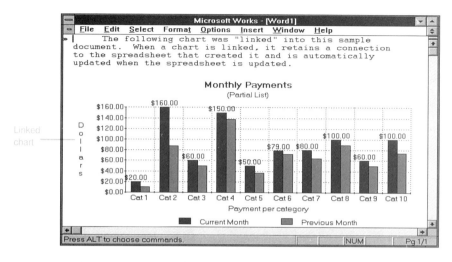

Figure 13.4   A linked chart is always kept up to date.

Note: To edit an embedded object, double-click on it. Works then loads the tool that created the object, and loads the object into it.

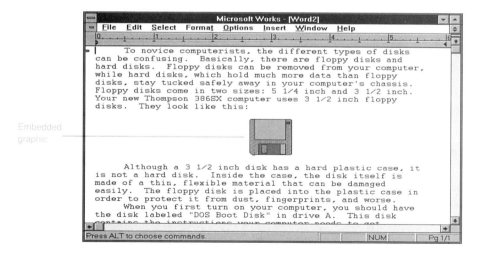

Figure 13.5   Drawings from Microsoft Draw are embedded into documents.

To embed a drawing, open the word processor document and position the text cursor where you want the drawing placed. Then, select Drawing from the Insert pull-down menu, which starts Microsoft Draw. Create your drawing, or import an existing drawing. When the drawing is ready, select Exit And Return from the File menu. Works asks whether you want to update your word processing document. Select the Yes button.

The following Quick Steps summarize how to embed a drawing into a word processor document.

 Embedding a Drawing into a Word Processor Document

1. Open the word processor document.

   Works loads the document into the active window.

2. Position the text cursor where you want the drawing placed and select Drawing from the Insert pull-down menu.

   Works starts Microsoft Draw.

212

3. Create the drawing or import an existing drawing from the File menu.

   If you import an existing drawing, Works loads it into the active window.

4. Select Exit and Return from the File menu.

   Works asks whether you want to update your word processing document.

5. Select the Yes button.

   Works embeds the drawing into your document.

When you have the drawing embedded into your document, you can later modify it by double-clicking on it, which causes Works to load the drawing into Microsoft Draw.

> **Tip:** If you select Draft view in the Options menu, the charts and drawings contained in a word processor document will be shown as outlines, rather than fully developed graphic objects, which speeds the redrawing of the screen.

> **FYIdea:** By taking advantage of data sharing, you can create comprehensive reports with little effort. Periodic reports can be revised quickly and easily using these features.

Changing an Object's Size

When Works adds objects to your documents, it chooses what appears to be an appropriate size, but you can easily make the objects larger or smaller. To do this, highlight the object, and select the object, then Picture from the Format menu. When the Picture dialog box appears (see Figure 13.6), type in the new measurements as percentages. That is, to make an object half size, enter 50 into both the Height and Width text boxes, or to make the object double size, type 200 into the height and width text boxes. After entering the new size, select the OK button or press Enter. Works resizes the object according to the measurements you entered.

213

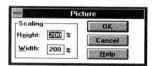

Figure 13.6   The Picture dialog box lets you change the size of objects.

Copying and Deleting Objects

Objects in a word processor document can be copied and deleted just like any other element of your document. To do this, just select the object (see Figure 13.7), and then select Copy, Cut, or Delete from the Edit menu, or press Ctrl+C, Ctrl+X, or Delete. After copying or cutting an object, you can paste it into another part of your document by selecting Paste from the Edit menu, or by pressing Ctrl+V.

Creating Form Letters

An extremely useful application made possible by shared data is the creation of form letters. By creating a general letter, and then using fields from a database for the heading and greeting of the letter, form letters, and other similar documents, are a snap to put together.

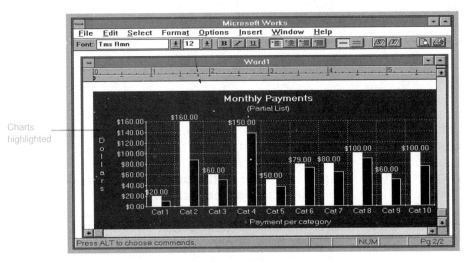

Charts highlighted

Figure 13.7   After highlighting an object, you can cut, copy, or delete it.

Before you can create form letters, however, you must have created a database of addresses. You can create the database form quickly by using the address-book WorksWizard, or you can use any existing database that contains the names and the addresses of the people to whom you want to send the letter or form.

After you create the database, you must create the letter, using the word processor. In this document, you should type only the text that is to be duplicated in every letter. In other words, don't add names or addresses at this point. You'll do that using fields from your database.

When your letter or form is ready, all you need to do is enter place holders where you want fields of your database printed (see Figure 13.8). You do this by selecting Database Field from the Insert pull-down menu, and selecting the desired field from the dialog box that appears.

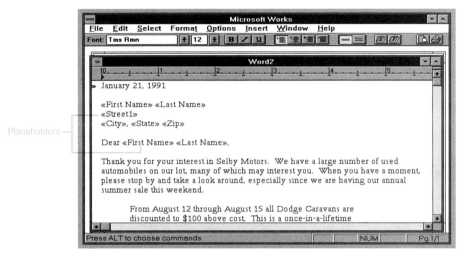

Placeholders —

Figure 13.8   Place holders let you define where fields from a database will be placed in a form letter.

215

The following Quick Steps guide you through the form-letter process.

 Creating Form Letters

1. Open the database containing the names and addresses of the people to whom you want to send the letter.

    Works loads the selected database into a window.

2. Open the letter document.

    Works loads the document into the active window.

3. In the letter, position the text cursor where you want the first line of the heading (in a business letter, the first line would be the person's name), and then select Database Field from the Insert menu.

    The Insert Field dialog box appears.

4. In the Databases list box, select the database that contains the names and addresses you want to use.

    Works highlights your selection.

5. In the Fields list box, select the field you want to insert into the letter.	Works highlights the selected field.
6. Select the OK button.	Works inserts the field's place holder into your document.
7. Type any text that you want to appear after the place holder.	The text appears in your document.
8. Repeat steps 4 through 8 for other fields you want to add.	Works adds the selected field place holders. □

After you've added all the place-holder fields you need, you should save the document so it'll be ready to use whenever you need it. When you've got your document safely tucked away on disk, you can print your form letters. To print your letters, use the following Quick Steps.

 Printing Form Letters

1. Open both the letter document and the database.	Works loads the two documents into their windows.
2. Select Print Form Letters from the File pull-down menu.	The Print Form Letters dialog box appears (see Figure 13.9).
3. In the Database list box, select the database containing the names and addresses you want to use.	Works highlights your selection.
4. Select the Print button.	The Print dialog box appears.
5. Make any necessary changes and select the OK button or press Enter.	Works prints the form letters. □

Creating Mailing Labels

Creating mailing labels is a lot like creating form letters. The difference is that, rather than typing a letter, all you put in the document is place holders for names and addresses (see Figure 13.10). To do this quickly, you can use the mailing-labels

WorksWizard by selecting <u>N</u>ew File from the File menu, and then
selecting WorksWi<u>z</u>ards from the Create New File dialog box. If you
want to use a database with different field names than those required
by the WorksWizards, however, you must create your label document manually.

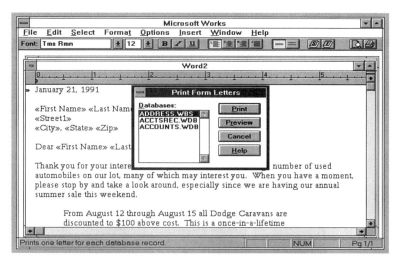

Figure 13.9 The Print Form Letters dialog box lets you
select the database that contains the names and addresses
you want to use.

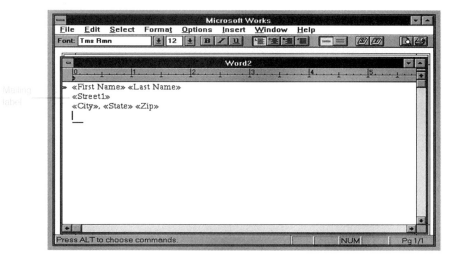

Figure 13.10 A mailing label document comprises only
address place holders and the text needed to format them
properly.

To create labels, start a new document, and then add database field place holders as described earlier in the section, "Creating Form Letters."

To print your labels, open both the label document and the database containing the names and addresses you want to use. Then, select Print Labels from the File pull-down menu. When the Print Labels dialog box appears (see Figure 13.11), select the database that contains the names and addresses you want to use in the Databases list box. Also, in their appropriate text boxes, type the height and width of your labels, as well as the Number of labels across page. Next, select the Print button. When the Page Setup & Margins dialog box appears, check that the page settings are what you want, and then select the OK button or press Enter. When the Print dialog box appears, select the OK button or press Enter.

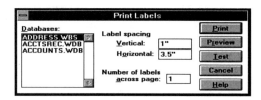

Figure 13.11   The Print Labels dialog box lets you choose a database, as well as set the size of your labels.

Use the following Quick Steps to implement the label-printing procedure.

 Printing Mailing Labels

1. Open both the label document and the database containing the names and addresses you want to use.	Works loads the two documents into their windows.
2. Select Print Labels from the File pull-down menu.	The Print Labels dialog box appears.
3. In the Databases list box, select the database that contains the names and addresses.	Works highlights your selection.

4. Press the Tab key and type the height of your labels. (If you're using standard 1" high labels, you can leave the default entry as is.)

The height you type appears in the Vertical text box.

5. Press the Tab key again and type the width of your labels. (If you're using standard 31/2" wide labels, you can leave the default entry as is.)

The width you type appears in the Horizontal text box.

6. Press the Tab key once more and type the number of labels across the label page.

The labels-across number appears in the Number of labels text box.

7. Select the Print button.

The Page Setup & Margins dialog box appears.

8. If the page settings are okay, select the OK button or press Enter. Otherwise, change the page settings to their correct values, then select OK.

The Print dialog box appears.

219

9. Select the OK button or press Enter.

Works prints your labels.

☐

Creating Envelopes

If your printer can handle envelopes, you can save more time by printing the names and addresses in your database directly onto envelopes, and so avoid pasting labels. Making envelopes is similar to creating labels (see Figure 13.12).

To create envelopes, open a new word processor document by selecting Create New File from the File pull-down menu. Then, if you're not using pre-printed envelopes, type your return address, pressing Shift+Enter after each line except the last. Press Enter until you're on the line where you want the destination address. Move the left margin marker to the right, to indent the destination address to its correct horizontal position, and insert database place holders for the destination address. When all needed place holders are inserted, select Page Setup & Margins from the File pull-down menu, and when the dialog box appears, change the document size to match the size of your envelopes. Also, change the margin size so the return address prints in the correct position. Finally, select the OK button or press Enter.

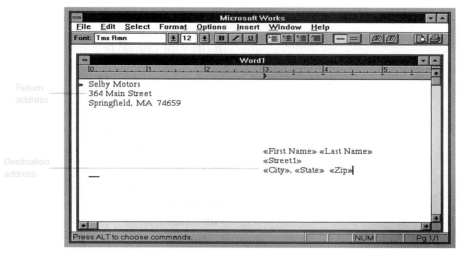

Return address

Destination address

Figure 13.12   Envelope documents are a little more complicated than mailing labels.

The following Quick Steps summarize this procedure.

 Making Envelopes

1. Open a new word processor document for your envelope by selecting Create New File from the File pull-down menu.

   Works opens a window for the new document.

2. Type your return address, pressing Shift+Enter after each line except the last. (If you're using envelopes that already have your return address printed on them, you should skip this step.)

   The text you type appears in the document.

3. Press Enter the number of times required to get to the line on which you want the destination address.

   Works moves the text cursor down once for each Enter.

4. Move the left margin marker to the right, to where you want the destination address.

Works indents the paragraph.

5. Using the procedure described in the previous sections, insert database place holders for the destination address.

Works inserts the selected place holders into the envelope document.

6. Select Page Setup & Margins from the File pull-down menu.

The Page Setup & Margins dialog box appears.

7. Change the document size to match the size of your envelopes, and change the margin size so that the return address prints in the correct position.

The new values you type appear in the appropriate text boxes.

8. Select the OK button or press Enter.

Your envelopes are ready to print. □

221

After creating your envelope document, you should save it to disk so it is available whenever you need it. Once you've saved the envelope document, you can print your envelopes, using the same procedure you used to print form letters. If, when you try to print the envelopes, Windows warns you that the Page size and orientation for your document do not match those of your printer, ignore the message and continue by selecting the Continue button.

The Database and Shared Data

Although it's less useful, you can copy data, with the exception of charts or drawings, from other tools into your databases. A paragraph or line of text copied from a word processor document can be copied into a single field of a record. If the text is over a certain length, it may be continued in the next record. When you copy data from a spreadsheet into a word processor document, the contents of each cell are placed in a separate field of the database, with each row of cells forming a new record.

> **Note:** You cannot paste charts or drawings into a database.

The Spreadsheet and Shared Data

There may be times when you want to copy text from a word processor document or fields from a database, into a spreadsheet document. When you copy text from a word processor document, it is placed in the selected cell of the spreadsheet, unless the text is in table form, with each entry separated by tabs. In this case, each table entry is placed in its own cell. When you copy data from a database, each field is placed into its own cell.

What You Have Learned

- ▷ Data can be added to a document as a copied, linked, or embedded object.
- ▷ When you copy data from a database into a word processor document, it is formatted as a table, with tabs between each field.
- ▷ Spreadsheet data is also copied into a word processor document in table form, with tabs between the contents of each cell.
- ▷ When you link spreadsheet data into a word processor document, the data in the word processor document changes when the source data changes.
- ▷ Spreadsheet charts can also be linked into a word processor document.
- ▷ When you add a drawing to a word processor document, it is added as an embedded object.
- ▷ By selecting Picture from the Format menu, you can change the size of a linked or embedded object.

► You can use the standard copy, cut, and delete functions on objects.

► By combining a word processor document with an address-book database, you can create form letters, mailing labels, and envelopes.

► Although it's less useful than copying data into a word processor document, you can also copy data from other tools into spreadsheets and databases. This data is copied, not linked.

223

Appendix A

Installing Works for Windows

Works comes on both high-density 5 1/4" and 720k 3 1/2" floppy disks. One of these sets must be transferred to your hard disk before you can run the program. Because the programs and data on the disks have been compressed to save space, you must use Microsoft's installation program to install Works. Simply copying the disks to your hard drive will not work.

> **Tip:** The Setup program takes quite a while to install Works. Don't get nervous if your system sometimes seems to be napping. There's a lot of data to be transferred.

To install Works for Windows onto your hard drive, first start your computer system and run Windows. When the Windows main screen appears, insert the Works Setup and Help disk into drive A. Then, from the Windows Program Manager, select Run from the File menu. When the Run dialog box appears, type `a:setup` and press Enter. The Works Welcome dialog box appears (see Figure A.1). Select the Continue button. When the Registration dialog box appears, type your name and company into the Registration text boxes, and select the Continue button. In the Setup Options dialog box, select the Complete Installation button. The Microsoft Setup program then copies files from the floppy disk to your hard disk. When the setup program prompts you for a new disk, replace the disk in drive A with the requested disk.

225

Figure A.1   The Microsoft Works Setup program installs Works onto your hard drive.

226

Use the following Quick Steps to install Works for Windows.

 Installing Works for Windows

1. Start your computer system and run Windows.	The Windows main screen appears on your screen.
2. Insert the Setup and Help disk into drive A.	You're now ready to run the installation program.
3. From the Windows Program Manager, select Run from the File menu.	The Run dialog box appears.
4. In the dialog box's text box, type **a:setup** and press Enter.	The Setup program runs and the Microsoft Works Setup screen appears.
5. When the Welcome dialog box appears, select the Continue button to install Works for Windows.	The Registration dialog box appears.
6. Type your name and company (if applicable) into the Registration text boxes, and select the Continue button.	The Setup Options dialog box appears.

7. Select the Complete Instal-   The Microsoft Setup
   lation button.   program starts copying files
                                       from the floppy disk to your
                                       hard disk.

8. When the setup program   The setup program copies all
   prompts you for a new disk,   the files from each disk.
   replace the disk in drive A
   with the requested disk.   □

Tip: You can install Works into a directory other than
C:\WINWORKS by clicking on the Custom Installation
button in step 7 above. This option also allows partial installation, where you select only specific files to copy. In addition,
you can install Works from drive B by substituting B for A in the
instructions above.

227

Topics for Further Study

Because *The First Book of Works for Windows* is a beginning tutorial, it doesn't include descriptions of some less-used Works functions. These functions, however, are covered thoroughly in your Works manual. When you are comfortable with the contents of this book, you will have a solid understanding of the Works for Windows tools. At that time, you may want to consider exploring advanced procedures not included in this book. Below is a list of topics you may want to investigate further by looking them up in your Works for Windows manual.

Common Tool Features

- ▶ Changing Works' default settings.
- ▶ Header and footer paragraphs.
- ▶ Adding page breaks.
- ▶ Dialing telephone numbers.
- ▶ Setting which files to open when starting Works.

The Word Processor

▶ Viewing two parts of a document simultaneously.
▶ Setting hanging and nested indents.
▶ Making text superscript, subscript, or strikethrough.
▶ Bookmarks.
▶ Creating document templates.

Microsoft Draw Chapter

▶ Editing the palette.
▶ Hiding and showing the palette.

The Database

▶ Viewing different parts of a database simultaneously.
▶ Creating default data entries.
▶ Handling records in List view.
▶ Advanced database querying.
▶ Protecting a database.
▶ Creating a template document.

The Spreadsheet

▶ Automatically entering a series of numbers and dates.
▶ Using the Paste Special command.
▶ Simultaneously viewing different parts of a spreadsheet.
▶ Manual calculation.
▶ Protecting entries.

Data Sharing

▶ Editing data links.

▶ Sharing information with other Windows applications.

231

Index

235

G

238

239

M

mailing labels
   creating, 216-218
   printing, 218-219
margins, 73-75
markers, changing in charts,
   197-199
mathematical operators,
   formulas, 108
MAX function, 146, 165
Maximize buttons, 23-25
Menu bar
   spreadsheets, 156-157
   Works screen, 10
menus
   Control, 23-25
   Format, 46-47
   Help, 10-11
   Pattern, 88-89
   Window, 26-28
Microsoft Draw, 4-5
   embedding drawings into
     word processor, 210-212
   exiting, 95
   fill patterns, 88-89
   importing pictures, 93-94
   line styles, 89
   objects
     aligning, 85-86
     copying, 86-88
     cutting, 86-88
     deleting, 86-88
     filled, 84-85
     flipping, 89-91
     framed, 84-85
     grouping, 91-93
     pasting, 86-88
     rotating, 89-91
   starting, 80

tools
   Arc, 83
   Arrow, 80-81
   Box, 83
   Ellipse, 82
   Freehand, 83
   Line, 82
   Rounded Box, 83
   Text, 84
   Zoom, 81-82
Microsoft Solution Series, 1
MIN function, 146, 165
Minimize buttons, 23-25
MOD function, 165
moving
   between fields, 108-109
   cells, 173
   fields, 104
   tabs, 55
   text blocks, 39

N

Name Chart dialog box,
   186-187
Name Report dialog box, 152
naming
   cells, 179-180
   charts, 186-187
   ranges, 179-180
non-recalculating values,
   160-162
nonadjacent values, charting,
   185-186
notes, entering in databases,
   122-123
NOW function, 165
NPV function, 165
number values, 159-162
numbers, entering in
   databases, 107-108

241

editing, 33
entering
   in databases, 106-107
   in spreadsheets, 159
inserting, 34
italic, 49-50
typing over, 34-35
underlined, 49-50
Text tool, Microsoft Draw, 84
Thesaurus, 64-65
Tile function, 27
time
   entering in databases, 122
   formats, 160-161
   values, 159-162
Time/Date dialog box, 122
titles
   adding to charts, 190
   deleting from charts, 190
Titles dialog box, 190
Toolbar
   database, 99
   fonts, changing, 47
   spreadsheets, 156-157
   Works screen, 10
tools
   database, 6
   Microsoft Draw, 4-5
   selecting, 8-10
   spreadsheet, 6-7
   starting, 8-10
   word processor, 3-4
   WorksWizards, 7-8

U

underlined text, 49-50
Undo function, 39-40
unhiding
   fields, 128
   records, 127-128

244

V

VAR function, 146, 166
vertical axis, changing in
   charts, 195-196
Vertical Axis dialog box,
   195-196
viewing
   charts, 187-188
   databases, 100-101
   documents, 25-26
   footnotes, 69
   gridlines, 157-158
   special characters, word
     processor, 42-43
   spreadsheets, 157-158
VLOOPUP function, 166

W

width, changing in cells,
   174-175
Window menu, 26-28
windows
   hidden, viewing, 27
   size, changing, 27
   switching between, 26-27
   see also, document windows
word processor, 3-4
   borders, 69-70
   character sizes, 48
   copying
     database data, 205-206
     objects, 213
     spreadsheet data, 206-208
   deleting objects, 213
   documents, creating, 32-33
   embedding drawings,
     210-212
   first-line indenting, 52-53
   fonts, 46-47
   footers, 65-67

footnotes, 68-69
headers, 65-67
line spacing, 53-54
lines, 69-70
linking spreadsheet charts,
   209-210
paragraphs
   indenting, 51-52
   spacing, 54
special characters,
   inserting, 60-61
   viewing, 42-43
spell checking, 61-64
starting, 32
tabs, 55-56
text
   aligning, 50
   bold, 49-50
   deleting, 35-36
   editing, 33
   inserting, 34
   italic, 49-50

replacing, 41-42
searching, 41-42
typing over, 34-35
underlined, 49-50
text blocks
   cutting, 38
   highlighting, 36-37
   moving, 39
   pasting, 38
Thesaurus, 64-65
Undo function, 39-40
Works for Windows
   installing, 225-227
   quitting, 11-12
   starting, 1-2
Works Welcome dialog box,
   225-226
WorksWizards, 7-8

Z

Zoom tool, Microsoft Draw,
   81-82

245

Sams Guarantees Your Success In 10 Minutes!

The *10 Minute Guides* provide a new approach to learning computer programs. Each book teaches you the most often used features of a particular program in 15 to 20 short lessons—all of which can be completed in 10 minutes or less. What's more, the *10 Minute Guides* are simple to use. You won't find any "computer-ese" or technical jargon— just plain English explanations. With straightforward instructions, easy-to-follow steps, and special margin icons to call attention to important tips and definitions, the *10 Minute Guides* make learning a new software program easy and fun!

10 Minute Guide to WordPerfect 5.1
Katherine Murray & Doug Sabotin
160 pages, 51/2 x 81/2, $9.95 USA
0-672-22808-4

Look to Sams for THE BEST
in Computer Information!

The Best Book of MS-DOS 5
Alan Simpson
650 pages, 73/8 X 91/4, $24.95 USA
0-672-48499-4

The Best Book of Harvard Graphics
John Mueller
400 pages, 73/8 X 91/4, $24.95 USA
0-672-22740-1

Look For These Books In Sams' Best Book Series

The Best Book of AutoCAD
Victor Wright
800 pages, 73/8 X 91/4, $34.95 USA
0-672-22725-8

**The Best Book of Lotus 1-2-3
Release 2.3**
Alan Simpson
850 pages, 73/8 X 91/4, $26.95 USA
0-672-30010-9

**The Best Book of Lotus 1-2-3
Release 3.1**
Alan Simpson
750 pages, 73/8 X 91/4, $27.95 USA
0-672-22713-4

The Best Book of Microsoft Windows 3
Carl Townsend
440 pages, 73/8 X 91/4, $24.95 USA
0-672-22708-8

**The Best Book of Microsoft Works
for the PC, Second Edition**
Ruth K. Witkin
500 pages, 73/8 X 91/4, $24.95 USA
0-672-22710-X

The Best Book of WordPerfect 5.1
Vincent Alfieri, revised by Ralph Blodgett
800 pages, 73/8 X 91/4, $26.95 USA
0-672-48467-6

SAMS

See your local retailer or call 1-800-428-5331.

Sams' Series Puts You "In Business"

The *In Business* books have been specially designed to help business users increase their productivity and efficiency. Each book comes with a companion disk that contains templates for common business tasks, as well as tear-out quick references for common commands. In addition, the books feature Business Shortcuts—boxed notes and tips on how to improve the performance of the software. Regardless of the size of the business or the level of user, these books will teach you how to get the most out of your business applications.

Quattro Pro 3 In Business
Chris Van Buren
400 pages, 7³/8 x 9¹/4, $29.95 USA
0-672-22793-2

Lotus 1-2-3 Release 2.3 In Business
Michael Griffin
400 pages, 7³/8 x 9¹/4, $29.95 USA
0-672-22803-3

Harvard Graphics 2.3 In Business
Jean Jacobson & Steve Jacobson
400 pages, 7³/8 x 9¹/4, $29.95 USA
0-672-22834-3

Q&A 4 In Business
David B. Adams
400 pages, 7³/8 x 9¹/4, $29.95 USA
0-672-22801-7

WordPerfect 5.1 In Business
Neil Salkind
400 pages, 7³/8 x 9¹/4, $29.95 USA
0-672-22795-9

See your local retailer or call 1-800-428-5331.

Turn to Sams For Complete
Hardware and Networking Information

The Business Guide to Local Area Networks
William Stallings
400 pages, 73/8 X 91/4, $24.95 USA
0-672-22728-2

LAN Desktop Guide to Printing with NetWare
Donna J. King
350 pages, 73/8 X 91/4, $39.95 USA
0-672-30084-2

More Hardware & Networking Titles

The First Book of Personal Computing Second Edition
W.E. Wang & Joe Kraynak
275 pages, 73/8 X 91/4, $16.95 USA
0-672-27385-3

The First Book of PS/1
Kate Barnes
300 pages, 73/8 X 91/4, $16.95 USA
0-672-27346-2

IBM PC Advanced Troublshooting & Repair
Robert C. Brenner
304 pages, 73/8 X 91/4, $24.95 USA
0-672-22590-5

IBM Personal Computer Troubleshooting & Repair
Robert C. Brenner
400 pages, 73/8 X 91/4, $24.95 USA
0-672-22662-6

Interfacing to the IBM Personal Computer, Second Edition
Lewis C. Eggebrecht
432 pages, 73/8 X 91/4, $24.95 USA
0-672-22722-3

LAN Desktop Guide to E-mail with cc:Mail
Bruce Fryer
350 pages, 73/8 X 91/4, $24.95 USA
0-672-30243-8

Microcomputer Troubleshooting & Repair
John G. Stephenson & Bob Cahill
368 pages, 73/8 X 91/4, $24.95 USA
0-672-22629-4

Understanding Local Area Networks, Second Edition
Stan Schatt
300 pages, 73/8 X 91/4, $24.95 USA
0-672-27303-9

SAMS

See your local retailer or call 1-800-428-5331.